CANAL WALKS

Nell Bridge lock, Oxford Canal (Walk 17)

Canal Walks
Vol 3. South

by
Dennis Needham

CICERONE PRESS
MILNTHORPE, CUMBRIA

ISBN 1 85284 227 X
A catalogue record for this book is available from the British Library.

Dedication
For Julie

Cicerone books by the same author:
Canal Walks Vol 1: North
Canal Walks Vol 2: Midlands

Front cover: The River Avon at Bath

CONTENTS

Advice to Readers

Readers are advised that whilst every effort is taken by the author
to ensure the accuracy of this guidebook, changes can occur which
may affect the contents. It is advisable to check locally on transport,
accommodation, shops etc. but even rights-of-way can be altered
and, more especially overseas, paths can be eradicated by landslip,
forest fires or changes of ownership.

The publisher would welcome notes of any such changes.

Introduction

Canal towpath walking. The ultimate escape into a world that has changed little in over 200 years. The routes and infrastructure are virtually as conceived. Only their users have altered.

The towpaths alongside most of England's canal system were originally built for use by horses, the initial motive power for boats. Most of our canals were constructed within thirty years either side of 1800, and provided cheap bulk transport at a time when this was unknown. Although much faster than the horse and cart and able to carry a vastly greater tonnage, the canals themselves fell victim to the search for increased speed and efficiency. Nineteenth century railways offered a more rapid service with much greater flexibility. With the arrival waterside of steam, soon followed by diesel power, the need for horse towpaths lessened and, in common with the accompanying water, maintenance was neglected.

Gradually falling into disuse, canals started to close. Many are now gone, leaving hardly a trace of their existence. However, soon after the last war, the Inland Waterways Association was founded to fight for the retention of these lengths of history. Under the enlightened leadership of Robert Aikman, campaigns to save threatened canals were mounted with a great degree of success. At that time, officialdom regarded canals as redundant and best filled in. Attending many public enquiries concerning the fate of these abandoned waterways, Aikman was able to demonstrate that it was cheaper to restore a canal than to infill it. This was not occasioned by financial legerdemain, but by arguing hard facts.

The renaissance of canals for recreational use has seen miles of towpaths reinstated which now provide hundreds of miles of good walking. Indeed, British Waterways themselves are responsible for over 1,500 miles, all in reasonable condition.

A generation ago the phrase "down by the canal" had connotations of grimy, rat-ridden old warehouses in the seedy part of town. Now, enlightened action by local and national bodies, both statutory and voluntary, often aided by local authorities, have transformed them - and our perception - into corridors of green, passing through some of the most beautiful scenery in this green and pleasant land, whilst giving city dwellers linear parks in which to linger.

From Essex to Lancashire, Yorkshire to Somerset, this great heritage is available to anyone who is able to walk for a couple of hours. There are no steep hills, although on some walks they crowd the water, almost giving the impression of fell walking. Equipped with nothing more than a pair of stout shoes - and the inevitable waterproof - they are there and available.

Their very nature as one-time transport arteries means that, although there are miles of greenery, the walks are never too far away from civilisation and its attendant public transport. This gives the walker the opportunity to head away from his/her car, confident that after a delightful and invigorating one-way walk, bus or train will return him/her to the car park.

This book follows a simple format. You are guided from a base point towards public transport that will convey you to the far end of the walk. From there, a walk back to the start can be undertaken at whatever pace suits. This eliminates the possibility of having to wait hours for the transport at the far end, to say nothing of the situation that once faced this writer when, after nine miles, the local bus drivers were found to be on strike. There is one circular walk, and a couple that do use transport for the return leg. There is always a good reason for this; see the text.

Most walks start at a point convenient to public transport and a car park. An Ordnance Survey grid reference is quoted for this location. A fact panel provides all the information needed before departure. Allow at least an hour for every two miles; there is always a view or building that simply demands a halt. Walks are grouped into chapters according to their area. The title "South" is a liberal interpretation, allowing the writer vast scope to select the finest walks available. Contrast the stark industrial buildings of central London with the wildness of Dartmoor, scene of the Tavistock walk. The majesty of Bath and the country homeliness of Kings Sutton. All are visited within these covers.

Pause and admire tunnels dug through solid rock without the aid of a single power tool, and delight at stone or brick built bridges, built for no other purpose than to allow farmers access to their fields that were severed when the canal was cut. Natural beauty is everywhere. Although many of the walks either begin or end in a town, there are miles of the most delightful countryside between: the Avon valley, rolling Cotswold hills, the coast at Bude, Hythe and Exeter, the mighty Severn valley or charming Oxfordshire villages. On a more bucolic note, a cow leisurely chewing its cud, peering over the parapet of a bridge, seems to add another dimension to canal walking.

Cities create their own fascination from the towpath. London, England's capital, is a fine example of "The Canal Effect". In a large city, the canal makes its entry through the back door, virtually ignored by residents.

How many people who live in the metropolis know that kingfishers, cormorants and kestrels live within a mile of Kings Cross station? They do and the walker is the most likely to see this manifestation. On the mammal side, fox and mink are city dwellers now; again, few people know.

This life is multiplied in the country. The scars of construction are now long gone, and many canals have a timeless feel to them. A full range of water fowl will be seen on canals, whilst rabbit, stoat, water vole and squirrel have taken up residence bankside. There is flora in abundance, many wild fruiting bushes and trees and enough butterflies to keep any lepidopterist in ecstasy. All canalside. Camera, binoculars and a bird identification book are all useful extras to a canal walk.

The OS Landranger series are invaluable maps for this kind of walking, but there are also canal cruising guides available. Usually at a scale of two inches to a mile, much of the information crammed between the covers is, perhaps, more relevant to boaters. But the walks will surely be augmented. Robert Nicholson Publications offer *The Ordnance Survey Guide to the Waterways* in five parts. Most of the walks in this book are to be found in the "South" edition, with only the non-navigable canals missing. Waterways World *Canal Guides* also offer invaluable snippets.

Although the walks are never too remote, the basic safety items carried by most sensible walkers are never out of place: compass, first aid, warm clothing, waterproofs, drink and a little energy food all fit into the smallest backpack, allowing the walker to face any situation with quiet confidence. One delightful aspect of these walks is that they pass a range of very congenial pubs. Many are still quite basic and most offer food, and the beer is always more palatable after a good walk.

As curiosity and interest is aroused by the waterways - as it surely will be - there are a number of books that will increase your knowledge. The most comprehensive coverage of history is recorded in a series of books by Charles Hadfield, published by David and Charles (of which Hadfield was once the "Charles"). Many are out of print now, but still obtainable through libraries. Three monthly magazines currently cover the subject: *Waterways World* caters for the more serious enthusiast, but in a very readable style; *Canal and Riverboat* takes a less traditional approach to the subject and is easily read. *Canal Boat & Inland Waterways* aims at newcomer and enthusiast alike and is very picture oriented. All these titles publish a canalside walk each month.

Finally, do not neglect the "green" aspect of canalside walking. Canals are man-made, although, 200 years along, it is difficult to believe. Towpaths were constructed to withstand the steady plod of thousands of horses, day in and day out. Accordingly, they do not show the kind of wear that is causing so much concern in many of our more popular walking areas. There is a warm satisfaction in knowing that after a good walk which has brought exercise, pleasure and fine scenery, you can retire to the fireside confident that your boots have done not the slightest damage to an otherwise frail environment. A comforting thought indeed.

So, lace up those boots, and try any of these thirty carefully selected walks. Then see how long it is before you are well and truly hooked on towpath walking.

WALK 1 - GUILDFORD TO GODALMING - WEY NAVIGATION

Godalming, a pleasant small commuter town set in deepest Surrey, has a particular place in waterway lore. It is the southernmost navigable point on the connected waterway system, lying at the south end of the Godalming Navigation, an extension of the River Wey. This was one of the first rivers to be equipped with pound locks when Sir Richard Weston was authorised to make the river to Guildford navigable in 1651, a feat he achieved two years later. The Guildford to Godalming section was not available to boats until 1760, but that still pre-dates most of the Midlands canal system. It carried large quantities of trade throughout the early years of the last century, this being enhanced by the opening of the Basingstoke Canal (see Walks 2 and 3) in 1796, and the Wey and Arun in 1816.

For many years the Stevens family owned the river before it was presented to the National Trust in 1964, as was the Godalming Navigation in 1968. They now administer and maintain the whole 19^1/$_2$ miles from the Thames southwards.

BEFORE YOU START

WALK DISTANCE:	5^1/$_2$ miles
MAP:	OS Landranger 196
START:	Godalming rail station
PUBLIC TRANSPORT:	Easy access from the whole rail system
STARTING GRID REF:	SU 967439
CAR PARKING:	At the station
TRANSPORT:	Excellent train service on Waterloo to Portsmouth via Havant line
REFRESHMENT:	Plenty of everything at each end. Pub with restaurant and tearoom with delightfully punnish name - By The Wey - at Farncombe

NEAREST TIC: 72 High Street, Guildford, Surrey GU1 3HE -
                    01483 444007

THE WALK

Leave Guildford station heading diagonally right towards Wey
House, beyond the traffic island. There is an underpass to help you
reach the far side of the road. Walk against the flow of traffic until
you reach the end of Wey House. Turn left, down to the river, and
turn right.

Guildford to Peasmarsh - 3 miles

After a few yards the towpath disappears for a short distance. There
is a well signposted walkway which soon returns to the waterside.
Generally speaking, Guildford does itself proud where it fronts the
river. Debenhams have an extremely pleasant shop with a riverside
restaurant and terrace outside giving excellent views over the
water. Plane trees and old-fashioned gas lamps adorned with
hanging baskets mark the walk, adding a somewhat pleasing
ambience. The Britannia Inn here offers Friary Meux beer for your
delectation, should you feel the need for refreshment before
embarking on your trek.

At the end of this promenade a bridge takes the path over water
to Mill Mead lock. Admire the elegant balance beams, made out of
old telegraph poles. A make-do-and-mend policy is often adopted
by the National Trust, who do not have the access to the maintenance
funds of British Waterways. Turn right, and follow the path alongside
what is now the Godalming Navigation. A hire base, Guildford
Boat House, is across the water. They offer steel hire boats, rowing
skiffs and a restaurant boat.

Sluices controlling the water levels in times of flood are bridged
before a sweeping right-hand turn takes the walk away from
Guildford. There is a bridge to the left here. Ignore it unless you
want to sample the delights of the Jolly Farmers which is across the
water on the apex of the bend. Guildford Rowing Club have a very
nice modern building across the river and you can often see its
members practising along the water. At the next bridge a public
footpath heads over to the left-hand side. Here, the North Downs
Way crosses the river. A 140 mile walk from Farnham to Dover, it

was originally Pilgrims Way, where Chaucer's Canterbury Pilgrims walked. A ferry once operated here, but is now long gone. The towpath stays on the right-hand bank for the whole of this walk.

An interesting hill just beyond this bridge has a rocky outcrop, some of which has turned into sand that has gently cascaded into the river, giving an ochre colour to the water. It is marked on the map as Sandy Corner: very apt. The towpath, which has been good so far, now starts to deteriorate, and by the time St. Catherine's lock is reached, it is not an easy walk, especially after heavy rain. The railway overhead is the line from Reading to Gatwick Airport, and is followed shortly by Guns Mouth, the start of the Wey and Arun Canal. The entrance, on the far bank, can still be seen, but the water and boat moorings last only a few yards.

Closed in 1871, after a mere 55 years of life, it was the central section of an ambitious scheme to link London and Portsmouth, avoiding the long journey down the Thames and through the Dover Straights. It was also to have strategic importance, allowing the passage of goods (and people) to Portsmouth without exposing them to the dangers of marauding foreign ships.

Hopes of moving up to 50,000 tons of freight a year never materialised, not even reaching 10 per cent of that. The

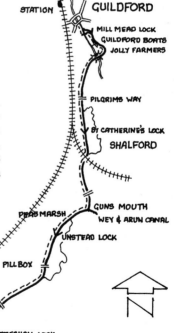

13

whole journey of 116 miles would have included 52 locks. Lack of water in the summit level of the canal, and the adjoining rivers, made passage something of a lottery. But, as is so often the case, plans are afoot to reopen it. The Wey and Arun Canal Trust, established in 1970, are hard at work carrying out physical restoration jobs and, more importantly these days, lobbying the decision makers. With the number of road crossings that will need reinstating, this aspect is crucial to the success of any project such as this. And success seems assured: reopening around 2010 is the current forecast.

Abutments of an old railway bridge are beyond. This carried a line from Guildford to Horsham through some really attractive countryside. It disappeared as part of the Beeching cuts in the 1960s. A private arm is next, with a pretty wooden bridge spanning it. A blue narrowboat moors here and, beyond, lawns lead up to a private house.

Peasmarsh to Godalming - 2½ miles

Unstead lock sees the start of a longish canalised section now; it is obvious by the straight course followed. A wartime pillbox, after the next road bridge, is preserved. It was one of over 5,000 built in the early 1940s, forming part of the Inland GHQ Defence line. This was the last of a number of defence lines protecting the capital and key industrial areas. It ran from the west coast near Bristol to the Kent coast near Chatham. Pillboxes took advantage of natural and manmade obstacles such as canals and rivers, and housed machine guns and anti-tank weapons.

The Manor Inn has a gate from the towpath into a garden, children's playground and the Beefeater Restaurant. They also serve morning coffee and offer accommodation. At Farncombe boathouse, by Catteshall Bridge, narrowboats are available for weekend or day hire throughout the year. The final lock on the navigation lies just above the road bridge, and the buildings of Godalming can now be clearly seen.

Approaching Godalming wharf, the river takes a sharp right-hand bend, revealing a length with some moored boats. Amongst these will be the answer to a question that had not consciously formed in your mind. This section of towpath is occasionally marked with horse manure, and the reason is the narrowboat *Iona*, a trip boat still powered in the traditional way.

Town Bridge is the effective end of navigation, though not the river. Cross that bridge to the left bank, and pick up a path through park alongside the river. It's a grassed area with plenty of mature willows. Right at the end is a huge gazebo, built in memory of John George Phillips, a native of Godalming, who was chief wireless operator on SS *Titanic*, and died at his post when the vessel foundered in mid Atlantic on 15 April 1912. The Postal Telegraphs Clerks Association provided a fountain and contributed towards the erection of the memorial.

At the next bridge come off the river and turn left. Immediately there is a sharp right down the newly built Vicarage Walk. At the far end a right and left give access to steps which leads up to the station car park.

WALK 2 - SEND TO SHEERWATER - RIVER WEY & BASINGSTOKE CANAL

A walk of pleasing contrasts, taking in the recently restored Basingstoke Canal and a section of the lower River Wey. Details of the river can be found in Walk 1, those of the canal in Walk 3.

BEFORE YOU START

WALK DISTANCE:	6½ miles
MAP:	OS Landranger Sheets 186 and 187
START:	Sheerwater Road, Sheerwater, Woking, Surrey
PUBLIC TRANSPORT:	West Byfleet station, on the Guildford to Waterloo via Woking line, is adjacent
STARTING GRID REF:	TQ 046617
CAR PARKING:	Plenty of on-street space
TRANSPORT:	London & Country service 563 operated by Surrey County Council between Addlestone and Guildford via Woking. Alternative service offered by same company on Heathrow Central to Guildford service 436, both operating on Sundays. Details on 01483 572137

| REFRESHMENT: | Pub at start, one en route, and all services within easy reach of finish |
| NEAREST TIC: | 72 High Street, Guildford, Surrey GU1 3HE - 01483 444007 |

THE WALK

Walk up Sheerwater Road to the T junction. Turn right into Woodham Lane, and the bus stop is around the corner after a few yards. Alight at the New Inn, Send.

Send to Walsham Flood Gates - 3 miles

The towpath is across the road from the New Inn on the left-hand side heading back the way you came. This section is an artificial channel known as Broadmead Cut. Much of the credit for making the Wey properly navigable is due to Sir Richard Weston. He lived a few miles south of here at Sutton Place, recently the home of Paul Getty. A Roman Catholic, Sir Richard fled to Holland at the outbreak of the Civil War in 1642. He became fascinated by the work of Dutch

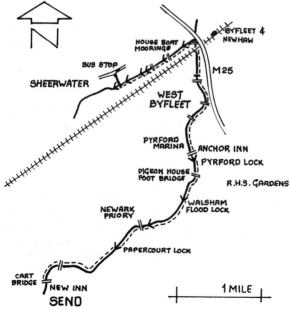

Old farm implements on display outside a very "des res" near Newark Lock, River Wey

drainage engineers, and on his eventual return to England in 1651 he obtained permission to improve the river to Guildford. This involved the construction of 12 locks and over 10 miles of canal.

Although no proof exists, there is good reason to suppose that he imported Dutch engineers to help. Support for the theory is enhanced by the existence locally of an area known as New Zealand, easily transmuted into Nieuw Zeeland, home for Dutch settlers. True? No-one knows for sure, but it does have a certain ring of authenticity, and is certainly accepted by those who never let facts get in the way of a good story.

At Papercourt lock, a very pretty stepped bypass weir returns the cut to the river. This is evident beyond as up to this point the walk has been alongside a neat towpath and bends have been orderly affairs. Now the river winds wildly, appearing to be searching for the Thames, but not quite sure which way to go. The towpath takes the right bank and there is occasionally deep mud at the edge of a field. At Newark New Bridge the river divides in two and the canal picks a course down the middle. Cross the road bridge to the left-hand side. A house on the right has a delightful collection of old horse-drawn farm implements on display. The remains of Newark Priory, a twelfth-century Augustinian Order, stands 100 yards to the left of this bridge, and is well worth the short detour needed to view.

The canal section is about 400 yards long, ending at Newark lock. From here, the towpath returns to the right bank along this river section which is almost a mile long. At the end, cross the sluices which bridge the river and lead to Walsham Flood Gates with its attractive cottage alongside. From here the walk is exclusively canal.

Walsham Flood Gates to Woodham Junction - 2½ miles

Below, to the right, in a deep cutting, and running very fast, the river almost forms rapids before curving away. The unusual waterside house on the left was once a lodge for Pyrford Place. This establishment achieved great notoriety a couple of centuries ago when owned by Sir Frances Dashwood (1701-1781), the 15th Baron le Despenser. Its association with the infamous Hellfire Club, John Wilkes *et al*, was a particularly rumbustious period of English history.

Beyond, the Anchor at Pyrford is a pub with restaurant and children's play garden. Boats congregate here on a warm summer weekend along with hordes of people watching the waterway activity; the place becomes quite frenetic. At quieter periods it is a charming spot to take a break. The entrance to Pyrford Marina is on the opposite bank, again, with boats moored both in the entrance and the lagoon beyond. Now the towpath is much improved. The waterside is piled, backfilled and covered with Thames valley sand; very good walking. Wisley Golf Club on the right has the distinction of being one of the most expensive clubs in England to join.

Essentially attractive, it's quite amazing how rural this walk still is, especially as the map indicates that the area is heavily developed. As ever, the water manages to avoid most manifestations of this. Gentle convolutions take the line northwards. The canal bridges are ancient and built from red brick, the parapets in various stages of disrepair. Horses graze the fields opposite, trees and water plants flourish and the bucolic scene could be rural England anywhere: until the egregious M25 arrives noisily from the right. Peace and tranquillity disappear, although the canal retains its rustic appearance amidst the mayhem. Then, to add to the cacophony, a railway bridge crosses overhead, carrying all the Waterloo traffic for Southampton, Bournemouth and Exeter, frequently augmented by suburban trains.

Woodham Junction to Sheerwater - 1 mile

At the junction with the Basingstoke Canal, pass under the railway bridge, and the steel footbridge which follows. This is a recent addition, erected in 1988 to link the towpaths of the two canals. Turn back onto this bridge and cross the water. Although this canal was only reopened to navigation in 1991, the towpath has been a popular local walk for many years. The canal is virtually straight along this length, and the first of six locks in the Woodham flight is reached after 300 yards. This was rebuilt in 1988, although work on the others had started back in 1975.

There are lots of houseboats in the first two pounds, many built on very ancient narrowboat hulls; loads of history here. There is even one wooden hull sitting sedately in a steel shell like an egg in an eggcup. The water is deep and clear, running in a pretty tree lined avenue. This is approaching the start of the Sheerwater area, now an industrial estate. It was 110 acres of lakeland until 1800, supplying fish commercially to London markets. The 7th Lord King took over in 1805, when they were infilled. A London County Council development hereabouts in the 1950s resulted in two years of continual pumping and pile driving before achieving a building base.

Lock 3 is particularly attractive, with a pretty lockside house. Here, a path to the left gives access to West Byfleet rail station. Just before lock 6 is a road bridge. This is Sheerwater Road, and the end of the walk.

WALK 3 - BROOKWOOD TO ASH VALE - BASINGSTOKE CANAL

Into the leafy backwaters of Surrey for an expedition along arguably one of the prettiest sections of canal anywhere in the country. This

The Basingstoke Canal Centre and offices at Mychett. (Walk 3)

is the recently restored Basingstoke Canal. Although there is no industry beside this walk, it is never far away from civilisation, and the towpath can get quite crowded at weekends.

The Basingstoke Canal was authorised by Act of Parliament in 1778, but the start was delayed for ten years by the country's parlous financial state caused by war. Work was completed in 1794 with the construction of 29 locks, 31 miles, and a troublesome 1,200 yard tunnel at Greywell. Commercially, it was a disaster from the outset, never making much money, and had a succession of owners, each of whom seemed to carry out the bare minimum of maintenance commensurate with the legal requirement to keep the canal open. The link to Basingstoke itself was lost as early as 1910. Mr A Harmsworth bought the canal in 1923 as part of his haulage business. He died in 1947 and the canal was bought on behalf of the Inland Waterways Association. Because of its run-down state, and the fact that it clearly would never operate again, the line was not nationalised in 1948.

The Surrey and Hants Canal Society was formed in 1966 with the aim of saving the, by now, defunct line. Theirs was a different plan to other restoration efforts around the country in that they sought to involve the local councils. Seven years of lobbying later, and after application for Compulsory Purchase Orders had been made, Hampshire County Council took over the section of canal within their boundaries. Surrey followed in 1976, restoration became possible, and work was soon under way. The line to the east of Greywell tunnel was reopened in 1991, and, should the bats who have taken up residence ever decide to leave their man-made cave, work will continue to the west with restoration of the collapsed eastern tunnel portal needed to link the navigable east with what remains of the west.

BEFORE YOU START

WALK DISTANCE:	6 miles
MAP:	OS Landranger Sheet 186
START:	Ash Vale rail station
PUBLIC TRANSPORT:	Good train service from Waterloo
STARTING GRID REF:	SU 892533
CAR PARKING:	Station car park
TRANSPORT:	Regular service Alton to Waterloo line
REFRESHMENT:	Pubs at each end, and one near Mychetts Place Bridge, almost at the end
NEAREST TIC:	Military Museum, Queens Avenue, Aldershot, Hants GU11 2LG - 01252 20968

THE WALK

Ash Vale station lies alongside the A321 Frimley and Camberley to Aldershot road in Surrey. Join the London-bound train to Brookwood, which is the first station, and alight there.

Leave the station from the northern platform (the one on which you arrive), walk down the approach and straight across the road is a narrow roadway, Sheets Heath Lane. Three hundred yards down there, a bridge takes the road across the canal. Turn left.

Brookwood to Deepcut Top Lock - 2½ miles

Pleasantly overgrown, this is excellent walking country. There are houses on the left, with occasional boats moored outside. Several wider sections contain the decaying branches of trees. These are home to the kingfisher population of this section of the Basingstoke

Canal, and the flash of electric blue as one of these delightful birds takes off is a sight to be coveted. They regularly perch here waiting for the unwary fish to swim past. Then, with a splash completely disproportionate to their size, they hit the water to capture another meal.

One mile along, Pirbright Bridge heralds the start of a flight of 14 locks which lift the canal almost 100ft. The towpath moves to the left-hand bank, reached by crossing the pretty little footbridge at the tail of lock 15. The locks themselves, with their traditional black and white paintwork, provide a delicious counterpoint to the natural colour and beauty of this flight. It is also one of the few canalside walks which offers gunfire as an integral part of its character. There are military rifle ranges here, and a huge barracks out of sight to the right. Also close by is the famous rifle range at Bisley. But the sound of mayhem all around does nothing to attenuate the extreme beauty of this walk. By now, the tone is firmly set with trees and thick bankside undergrowth.

Mature trees line both banks. Small basins below the locks, and greenery everywhere combine to add to the overall effect. Between locks 22 and 23, iron railings are still in place on the non-towpath side. The army used this area as a swimming pool earlier this century. Swimming was stopped when the men started to go down with polio, but the

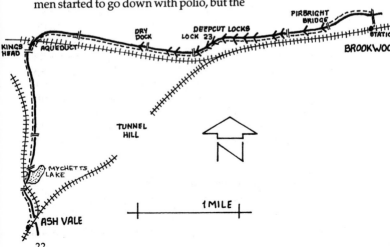

locals who also swam there were unaffected. The problem was eventually traced to the camp's drinking water supply. The fence on the non-towpath side is a little forbidding with yards of fencing, security lights and barbed wire in place.

Deepcut Top Lock to Mychett Place - 2¹/₂ miles

The cottage alongside the top lock is a delightful place, seemingly remote but only a few yards away from civilisation. It was originally the location of a carpenter's shop, now occupied by one of the canal wardens, and the dry dock across the water was rebuilt in 1984 after having been infilled for almost half a century.

This is the start of Deepcut. With very little boating yet, and few walkers, this is simply exquisite. Over 1,000 yards long and up to 70ft deep, the sides slope away to provide good anchorage for a whole range of trees. Most of our native species can be found growing here, and the autumnal hues defy description in their beauty. And the names of land surrounding the canal are a source of much humour: Cuckoo Hill, Donkey Town, Colony Bog, Strawberry Bottom and Cow Moor are all within easy striking range.

A sweeping left-hand bend takes the canal to Frimley Aqueduct, which is actually a crossing of the railway. It was built when the London and Southampton Railway was constructed in the 1830s, and extended to its present size in 1900 when the railway company wanted to add additional tracks. A short distance beyond is Kings Head Bridge, where the towpath moves to the right bank. Leave the water by Frimhurst Lodge and walk up their drive to the road. Cross the narrow bridge, and regain the path on the right side. A short diversion is available here by walking beyond the towpath and down the hill to the Kings Head, a free house with a good range of traditional beers. There is also a Harvester Restaurant attached, but be warned: if you want to eat there on a Sunday, reservation is essential.

Mychetts Land Bridge to Ash Vale - 1 mile

The headquarters of the Basingstoke Canal Company can be seen on the far bank. Access is possible via the road bridge, and there is a small shop selling ice cream and goodies, with a display telling much of the canal's history.

Yet more woodland keeps an absolutely rural feel to this walk, a feeling that will last almost into Ash Vale. Mychetts Lane Bridge has been newly rebuilt, replacing a somewhat inadequate structure, and beyond is an expanse of water known as Mychetts Lake. A wire fence divides the canal from the lake. Here also is Mychetts Place, whose most recent claim to fame is that it was used as a prison for the Nazi leader Rudolf Hess for a period during the last war after his abortive flight to Scotland.

At last, the rural effect starts to recede. Houses and main road are an unwelcome intrusion after what has gone before. At the next (railway) bridge, a path leads to the right from the towpath down to the station, but before leaving, examine the rather functional warehouse that has an old handpainted sign attached by the New Basingstoke Canal Company giving their statutory warning. Here was one of the canal wharves that shared some of the sparse trade in years gone by.

One footnote. The effect of the seasons on this walk is dramatic. The fresh bright greens of early summer are followed by more mature shades as summer progresses; and then autumn is sheer magic; followed by the stark emptiness of winter. This is a walk that can be repeated *ad infinitum*, and will always look different. Try it the other way at different times of the year: you will not recognise it.

WALK 4 - ODIHAM TO THE HATCH - BASINGSTOKE CANAL

This walk reaches the westernmost extremity of this recently restored canal, then onwards to the yet-to-be-restored section and some of the never-to-be-seen-again length.

A look at the history of the birth, death and renaissance of this most attractive canal can be found in Walk 3.

BEFORE YOU START

WALK DISTANCE:	6 miles
MAP:	OS Landranger Series No 186
START:	The Hatch, Old Basing. This is on the main

	A30 London to Basingstoke road
PUBLIC TRANSPORT:	Good to Basingstoke
STARTING GRID REF:	SU 676521
CAR PARKING:	Side roads in Old Basing or at the Hatch pub - with permission
TRANSPORT:	Basingstoke to Camberley bus service 200 (not Sundays) operated by Stagecoach Hampshire. Details on 01256 464501
REFRESHMENT:	Excellent pub at the end of the walk, plenty of shops in Odiham, pub at start and one with a filling station shop en route
NEAREST TIC:	Willis Museum, Old Town Hall, Market Place, Basingstoke, Hampshire RG21 1QD - 01256 817618

THE WALK

A bus stop will be found across the main A30 at the Hatch pub, right outside a garage. Alight at the first stop beyond the centre of Odiham and walk back a few yards to turn right into a narrow lane. There is no name to this, but a signpost indicates that the Vine Church, Basingstoke Canal and Water Witch pub are down the

King John's Castle at North Warnborough on the Basingstoke Canal

road: they are. The latter is a few yards before the water and has an excellent garden with amusements for youngsters. One is a full size mock-up of a narrowboat, offering plenty of fun for would-be boat skippers. The pub serves food and has a good line in real ale.

A building between there and the bridge was once the canalside pub. Called the Cricketers then, it is a private house today. The gable wall still carries evidence of its past, advertising

CROWLEY & CO. LTD, ALTON ALES AND STOUT
AND FOREIGN SPIRITS

Odiham to Warnborough - 1¹/₂ miles

Cross the bridge and turn left along the towpath. There is a picnic site a couple of yards the other way. Immediately, the tenor of this walk is set. Completely rural, with scarcely a house to be sighted, it still suffers a modern-day blight, albeit intermittent and not too intrusive. There are several main roads using the same valley area as the canal, one of which is the M3 motorway, and noise from these sources can impinge on one's sensibilities and destroy the illusion of rurality.

There are several bridges, and a canal that insists on following a convoluted course, all adding to the overall interest. By the bridge in Warnborough, a flight of steps leads to a road. On the right, right alongside, is a filling station which offers basic sustenance, and a pub, the Swan, offering more substantial food.

Warnborough to Up Nately - 3¹/₂ miles

The walk is reaching the end of its navigable section now as, around a corner, right alongside the towpath, are the remains of Odiham Castle. Also known as King John's Castle, this is all that is left of a three-storey keep which formed part of the fortress built about 1207. King John used it as a stopping place between Windsor and Winchester. Here he would hunt or rest. It was also the point from which he set out for Runnymede to set his seal on Magna Carta in June 1215.

It was subsequently given to the widow of Simon De Montfort who had been killed at the Battle of Evesham. King David of Scotland was incarcerated here from 1347

to 1357. There is little recorded history during Tudor times and beyond, but when the canal came through here in 1792, the engineers severed the outer bailies and surrounding moats. What is left is listed as an Ancient Monument.

By the castle is a very pretty clear chalk stream arriving from the right into the canal, which widens appreciably at this point. This is a winding hole and marks the western limit of navigation. A seat is provided alongside the towpath, and beyond, the water is appreciably shallower with a heavy weed growth. Around here the towpath hedge is almost solid sloe bushes. A walk in September when the fruit is out is mandatory for those who make their own sloe gin. The lack of disturbance from boats also encourages bird life. Little grebe, duck and coots all live in his section.

Ahead lies the cause of the closure, Greywell Tunnel: 1,230 yards long, it was built between 1788 and 1792 to avoid a long detour around the hill. There was no towpath, so boats were legged through whilst the horses followed a route similar to the way this walk will go. The tunnel collapsed in 1932 and, as trade was already moribund, no attempt was made to repair it. From the tunnel westward, the canal was abandoned, that beyond Hatch, sold.

Even with the restoration climate existing today, Greywell is a non-starter. It is believed that some 300 yards of tunnel has fallen. And there is the question of the bats. The tunnel is of huge ecological importance as a haven for hibernating bats. It is the largest known bat roost in Britain and has the second largest population of Natterer's bats in the world. Due to its constant temperature, lack of draught and damp atmosphere, it is a perfect location and up to 12,000 take

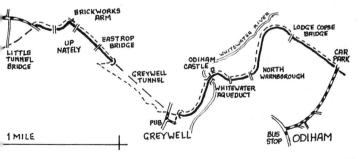

advantage of it each year. Not surprisingly, it is listed as a Site of Special Scientific Interest.

Walk up the path and turn left to cross over the mouth of the tunnel. This leads to a road and a junction. Turn right, noting that there is a pub, the Fox and Goose. Some 40 yards along on the left is a Public Footpath sign which is the walk. Follow this track gently uphill, swinging to the right as it does so. Then there are two junctions in quick succession. Ignore the first left, a crush, and take the second, a stile.

Walk across this field, keeping close to the left-hand fence, towards a house on the skyline. The path then meets another arriving from the left. Turn right across the field, aiming for a large oak tree. Past that tree, start bearing slightly left as the well worn path goes over a crest and down towards another oak tree and into woodland. A metal gate then bars the path, with a wooden gate a couple of yards to the right. Pass through here and down the path.

Some of these turns have had a hand painted white TUNNEL sign indicating the way, and the most important one is about $^1/_2$ mile along this path. It is broken, and points right, to a much lesser track. This is a Permissive Footpath, courtesy of the Greywell Hill Estate. Down here is the other end of the tunnel. This is in the process of being restored. Much of the masonry that was buried for years is now revealed, although there is little evidence of water.

The canal then moves in rapid succession from under restoration to disappeared completely to shallow ditch holding water except in high summer. There is a series of bridges, all in reasonable condition, one quite high as it strides over the canal which is in a cutting. Across a footbridge, the canal turns sharp left, with an old arm to the right. The towpath condition is variable along this section, but the canal company have ambitious plans to upgrade the whole length of it to a very high standard. It is not beyond the realms of possibility that this section will one day see boats again. There are various options under consideration to get round Grilles Hill, and once a plan is adopted and funds located... The canal bed reaches another winding hole, beyond which it is infilled.

Up Nately to the Hatch - $1^1/_2$ miles

Walk along what was the canal bed to a road and bear right,

effectively continuing to walk in the same direction. Follow the road as far as the motorway, and immediately on the left is a turn. Take this, and very soon, the walk returns to the Hatch pub.

WALK 5 - SANDGATE TO WEST HYTHE - ROYAL MILITARY CANAL

Kent has never been to the forefront canalwise. The only effective navigation is on the Medway - see Walk 4. But the longest artificial canal in the county was the Royal Military Canal.

The Royal Military Canal has its place in our history books not primarily as a method of transportation, but as an anti-invasion barrier. In 1804 the French under Napoleon were widely believed to be amassing an invasion fleet across the Channel. In the fond belief that they could counter the threat, the government, with a cavalier disregard for taxpayers' money, decided that a canal across the most likely landing place would defeat the invader. The fact that Napoleon had conquered half of Europe, crossing natural obstacles far greater than this, was not perceived as relevant.

The canal was built, and by the time it was finished the Franco-Spanish fleet had been well defeated at Trafalgar and the threat vanished. Result? One unused canal with no purpose in life. It was then decided to make it available for civilian use, and actually carry freight - albeit still under the control of the military, to whom maintenance duties were allotted. Commercial traffic started to use the water, although never in great quantity, until the arrival of a railway in the late 1840s saw what trade there was savaged.

In 1872 an Act of Parliament presaged the beginning of the end. Parts were either leased or sold, and the last recorded toll was collected in 1909. Since then, there have been several changes of ownership, but the integrity of the line has remained assured. Some sections can be used by boats, whilst walkers can access chunks of it without actually being able to walk the whole 22 mile length. One fascinating aspect of its construction is that it makes the whole of Romney and Walland Marshes - already reclaimed from the sea - into an island.

An ornate bridge crosses the Royal Military Canal at West Hythe, Kent

BEFORE YOU START

WALK DISTANCE:	5¹/2 miles
MAP:	OS Landranger Sheet 189
START:	West Hythe, 1 mile inland of the A259 Hythe to Dymchurch road
PUBLIC TRANSPORT:	Nearest railway is Folkestone
STARTING GRID REF:	TR 125342
CAR PARKING:	Car park alongside the canal bridge
TRANSPORT:	Stagecoach East Kent bus services 11, 12 and 12A travel the A259. Details from 01843 581333
REFRESHMENT:	Pub on first section, all services in Hythe, otherwise nothing
NEAREST TIC:	Prospect Road Car Park, Hythe, Kent CT21 5NH - 01303 2667799

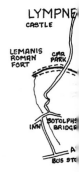

LYMPNE CASTLE

LEMANIS ROMAN FORT

CAR PARK

BOTOLPHS INN BRIDGE

A

BUS STC

THE WALK

Leave the car park and cross the ornate canal bridge, and walk along that road to a junction. Bear right, across a bridge and turn immediately left by the Botolphs Bridge Inn. When you reach the main road, almost 1 mile in all, the bus stop is close by.

Entering Seabrook, look out for a large garage selling Citroën cars. Immediately beyond is a bus stop. Alight here.

Sandgate to Hythe - 2½ miles

Walk back, crossing the road to the sea wall. Bear left just before the Murco filling station and Little Chef and along the seafront, Prince's Parade. After 75 yards cross the road, just beyond the 40mph sign, and a flight of steps leads off to the right down to the canal. Bear left around the actual outflow and turn right to pick up the towpath.

Initially, the canal looks slightly scruffy. It is below both the sea wall to the left, and the road to the right. Before long, however, things improve. The road moves away, and a 9 hole golf course can be seen to the left. A footbridge crosses the water and the huge Imperial Hotel stands proudly on the seafront a little to the left. The canal is still unkempt, but this is about to change dramatically as the walk arrives at Twiss Road bridge.

Cross this and enter the section owned by Hythe Council. Now the Royal Military Canal becomes the central feature of the town. The line is arrow straight, everything is clean, and the whole area takes on the appearance of a well landscaped ornamental lake. Even the towpath is paved. At the next bridge the Hythe Venetian Fete takes place biennially - on odd dated years. The name probably says

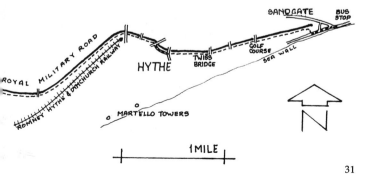

1 MILE

it all. It's a wonderful carnival with boats, entertainments and fireworks. It lasts all day and well into the evening and is held on the third Wednesday in August. Inevitably, its rarity ensures that the event draws a huge crowd - both locals who know what to expect, and holidaymakers who don't.

Hythe itself is a very ancient place. Mentioned in Domesday, it once had a harbour, and, as one of the Cinque Ports, was an integral part of our ancient defences. This confederation was formed by Edward the Confessor (1042 to 1066) and provided men and ships for defence of the country in return for exemption from some taxes, and the right to their own courts. The Warden, also Constable of Dover Castle, is a ceremonial role, currently held by the Queen Mother. Silting caused Hythe's harbour to become unusable by the fifteenth century, and there is no port here now.

Hythe to West Hythe - 3 miles

Beyond Stade Street bridge, the towpath disappears, but Portland Road runs alongside. Follow this and, as the canal swings round to the right, take a path that runs alongside but above the water, to the Dukes Head pub. Both liquid sustenance and food are available here. Cross the main road, and opposite is a gap in the wall leading to a paved path alongside the canal, still on the left-hand bank. At the end is the main road again. Cross, and regain the towpath. There is a café here and, a little to the left, the eastern terminus of the Romney, Hythe and Dymchurch Railway. At one-third normal size, this is the smallest public railway in the world. It runs from the terminus here to Dungeness lighthouse 14 miles along the coast. It operates during the summer months only, and has a splendid collection of both steam and diesel locomotives.

As the walk leaves the town, the ridge of hills on the right starts to dominate. The railway swings away to the left as the canal moves slightly right, passing under a low, girder construction footbridge. Two aspects of the military history of this water are to be seen now. The far bank is built much higher than necessary. This served a dual purpose. It provided a fine view over the plain towards the sea, one that could be well covered by the guns which were once located here. The other, more mundane but equally important strategically, was that men and munitions could be moved along the road behind

Deepcut Top Lock, Basingstoke Canal (Walk 3)
The River Medway at Tonbridge (Walk 6)

Newbury (Walk 8)
Dundas Aqueduct, Kennet & Avon Canal (Walk 11)

it, out of sight of any watching ships that might be out in the Channel.

Of course, that was the only way to garner intelligence then: spy satellites and reconnaissance aircraft were somewhat scarce in Napoleon's time! That said, the supremacy of the Royal Navy in those days was such that it would have taken a very determined (and lucky) French captain to get close enough for long enough to take a good look. The occasional bend in the course of the canal also had military significance. At these points were raised areas, again to accommodate defensive weaponry.

As the walk nears its end, the bulk of Lympne (pronounced Lim) Castle can be seen on the cliff edge. Alongside is the twelfth-century church of St. Stephen. At the termination of the walk it's worth summoning the energy to walk a little further along the towpath. Then you will come upon the site of the Roman port and fortress of Portus Lemanis. The very fact that it was located here gives a graphic illustration of how successful land reclamation schemes have been.

After completion of the walk, an uphill drive to the castle is well worth the time. The views over the coast and marshes are fantastic. It is possible to pick out several Martello Towers, another remnant of Napoleonic defences, on the seashore. Also to look out over Dymchurch and Romney Marsh, most evocative to those who have thrilled to the deeds of derring-do by the Scarecrow as told in Russell Thorndike's *Doctor Syn* books. These tales, so popular in the interwar years, were the subject of a film in 1962 with Patrick McGoohan as the eponymous hero, and George Cole as his rascally sidekick Mr Mipps, the verger.

The castle is privately owned, but is open to visitors. The east tower is of Norman origin, and the Great Hall has superb panelling. It was originally the Archdeacon's residence before being sold in 1870. Details of opening times are available on 01303 267571.

The church alongside is also basically Norman with a central tower. Internally, it is pleasant without ever being dramatic. The building suffered damage from a V1 "doodlebug" in August 1944. The stained glass in the eastern window was destroyed, and replaced in 1950. Outside, another connection with that war can be found. At the eastern end of the churchyard are graves of RAF pilots who fought the Battle of Britain.

WALK 6 - TONBRIDGE TO EAST PECKHAM - RIVER MEDWAY

To a navigable river now, many miles away from the connected system, and totally ignored by most waterside walkers. Flowing for some 70 miles through deepest Kent, the River Medway actually rises in three headstreams, two in Sussex and one in Surrey. The navigable length is generally reckoned to be 43 miles from Sheerness up to Tonbridge. Smaller boats with an air draught of around 5ft or less will extend this by over 2 miles, dinghies by almost 8 miles.

The river was made navigable in the 1740s by the Medway Navigation Company, but they ceased trading early this century. There is now no commercial traffic along this walk, but it is very popular with pleasure boats. One point to bear in mind before planning your visit is that this is a river navigation. After periods of prolonged rain, flooding is endemic on the towpath, and will cause problems. Also worthy of note is the fact that the towpath does not stick rigidly to the waterside, as a canal path does. Whilst never very far away, there are occasions when the flood banking, trees or undergrowth will obscure your view. But it's still a very worthwhile experience, and, although not as busy as, say, the Shropshire Union Canal, there are boats of all shapes and sizes and they do move, even in the winter.

BEFORE YOU START

WALK DISTANCE:	7 miles
MAP:	OS Landranger Sheet 188
START:	The Merry Boys Inn, Snoll Hatch Road, East Peckham, a Kent village almost halfway between Maidstone and Tonbridge to the east of the A26
PUBLIC TRANSPORT:	Nearest is Tonbridge
STARTING GRID REF:	TQ 667486
CAR PARKING:	Ample space in the surrounding streets
TRANSPORT:	Grey Green Coaches service 208 leaves for Tonbridge (not Sundays). Service details from 01634 713011

REFRESHMENT:	Every facility in Tonbridge, pub in East Peckham, nothing between
NEAREST TIC:	Castle Street, Tonbridge, Kent TN9 1BG - 01732 770929

THE WALK

Catch the bus to Tonbridge. Of no concern to the walk but of passing interest during the journey is the tiny village of Snoll Hatch. A "hatch" is the Anglo-Saxon word for a hitch gate, the entrance to a king's forest. This place had no less than 14 pubs in the last century, one of which, the Merry Boys, had its name transferred up the road when it closed in the 1930s.

Alight in the main street in Tonbridge at the stop just by the river. The bridge is a particularly attractive event, and the effective head of navigation is a few yards upstream of here where the waters divide. In the 1830s a scheme to extend the navigation to Penshurst, 8 miles, away was instigated. Some earthworks and two locks were partially constructed, but the work was never completed. There is a superb ruined Norman castle in Tonbridge that is well worth a visit.

Tonbridge to Eldridges Lock - 2 miles

Turn down Medway Wharf, past the Castle, a Courage pub. At the end of the post office building is a path to the left which leads to the River Medway Navigation. Turn right, and after 300 yards reach the

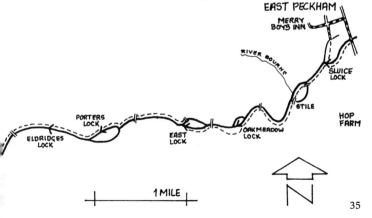

Town lock. There is a plethora of paddle gear attached to the gates; a very unusual appearance to those more used to standard canals. At the tail of this lock is a gate which leads to a paved public footpath. Follow this to the road bridge, and turn left, over the river, to regain the towpath which is now on the left shore. There is a public footpath down the right-hand side, but be sure to ignore it as this veers away from the river very shortly.

After the bridge the river widens into a water meadow, with pleasant views to each side and Tonbridge already behind. As the walk proceeds, the towpath, which was well maintained initially, deteriorates from paved through firm to a muddy morass in places. A high banking to the right needs closer examination: Eldridges lock is concealed there. A path leads over the banking to give a view of the complex arrangements that take the river around the lock.

Eldridges Lock to Sluice Weir Lock - 3½ miles

The valley is wide now, with agriculture to the fore. Through the distant trees ahead, the white tips of a group of oast houses can be seen. These are well distributed all over Kent and were once used to dry hops. All now redundant, they have mainly been converted to rather splendid living accommodation, and are invariably well kept. On the slope to the left side of the valley is the village of Hadlow, and the prominent building is a tall Gothic tower. This is a folly, built by Walter Barton May in 1835 at Hadlow Castle. It was originally 150ft high, the aim of its creator being to obtain sea views from his inland estate. Some of the top has now been removed. It is privately owned, and not open for visits.

The main course of the river takes a dive off to the right, dropping over its weir out of sight, whilst a channel takes the navigable section through Porters lock. As the walk nears those oast houses, a high hedge stands between them and the river. Behind are the tall trellises that carry the hop vines. Beyond, a bridge takes the walk over a modern sluice mechanism and to East lock. A further bridge at the tail carries the towpath to the right-hand bank.

The next bridge is a footbridge only and does not concern us, except to note that it carries the Wealdway, a long distance footpath, across the river. Beyond there, the wide open views come to an end as woodland takes over, offering a fine collection of traditional

English deciduous species; a wonderful sight, compounded in autumn by the magnificent range of hues as the leaves start to fall.

After a few yards in the trees, the towpath makes a slight diversion from the riverside: down off the flood bank to run about 20 yards from the water for the next 200 yards. Then, back up to the usual position. The trees recede as Oak Meadow lock hoves into view. At the next bridge the main path appears to cross: resist the temptation. Keep to the lesser track on the right bank, which will soon establish itself as a good towpath again.

A stile then guards a tiny footbridge over a very narrow reach. The land beyond is actually Bullen Island, which has an interesting story. It was arable farmland for many years. Then, when set-aside farming policy was just a twinkle in the eyes of the "Brussels bureaucrats", this island was left fallow. It is now a haven for both flora and fauna. There is a very good chance of a kingfisher sighting here, and woodpeckers can often be heard tapping out their frenetic Morse code. Altogether a delightful, unsung nature reserve, made all the healthier because it is not affected by the grass cutting rules that insist on driving a mower across fields when the inhabitants are in the middle of their reproductive phase. Across the way, the River Bourne empties its contribution in the Medway.

Sluice Weir Lock to East Peckham - 1½ miles

The path crosses over the sluice to the lockside, and then back again to the towpath, still on the right. If a shortened walk is preferred, it is possible here to take the path that crosses the head of the lock, walk up to the road and turn left. This will reduce the walk by something less than a mile.

The last section of the walk takes in Sluice Weir lock. It's hard to imagine now, but East Peckham was a thriving inland port once upon a day. But river navigations, in common with canals, suffered from the arrival of railways, and went into parallel decline. For the record, the pound here is over 30ft lower than when the walk started, and less than 30ft above sea level; the first lock at Allington being just over 11 miles away. Another 600 yards or so sees the path arrive in a car park by a tiny industrial area. Pass through this to the road, turn left, cross the river, and turn left again beyond the Rose and Crown into Old Road which will return you to the Merry Boys and your car.

With the time - and inclination - it is possible to extend the walk by over $1/2$ mile. Turn right on leaving the water, and $1/4$ mile down the road on the left is the Whitbread Hop Farm. This is an exposition of hop growing, gathering and drying. To augment this fascinating story, the famed Whitbread Shire horses are based here and there is an animal village with a collection of birds of prey. It's open all year and there is an admission charge. Full details are available on 01622 872068.

Chapter 2:
Kennet and Avon Canal

WALK 7 - READING TO ALDERMASTON - INCLUDING THE RIVER THAMES

Concomitant with the restoration to navigation of this 75 mile long canal, the towpath has been reinstated for almost the whole length and offers some beautiful walking. The paucity of public transport excludes some of the line, but what is left is exciting, beautiful and occasionally dramatic.

The original concept was for a canal to link London with Bristol. Trade between the two cities was either by very poor roads, or coaster. This involved a passage around Land's End with its treacherous seas, and a canal would revolutionise this. The eastern end of the Kennet and Avon was one of the earlier canalised rivers in the country, being opened as far as Newbury in 1723. It was the section of turf sided locks, those peculiar structures that are now almost a fond memory, although restoration has recreated some of them to a degree. Navigation from Hanham on the River Avon to Bath was possible by 1727, but the link between was not completed until 1810. Seventy-nine locks, two grand aqueducts and a tunnel were needed before the 57 miles between Newbury and Bath, engineered by James Rennie, were opened.

Trade was excellent in the early years, but competition from the railways was soon felt. The Great Western Railway bought the canal in 1852 and did absolutely nothing to encourage trade. By the time the twentieth century had dawned, navigation was already difficult with a huge backlog of maintenance.

After the last recorded through passage in 1951, closure proposals were made, but an active Canal Association, a branch of the Inland Waterways Association, which became the Kennet and Avon Trust in 1962, fought them with great success, instigating a programme for through restoration which was finally to come to glorious fruition on 8 August 1990 when the Queen reopened the whole canal at a ceremony in Devizes - see Walk 8.

BEFORE YOU START

WALK DISTANCE:	11 miles
MAP:	OS Landranger Sheet 175
START:	Aldermaston rail station, just south of the A4 Great West Road
PUBLIC TRANSPORT:	Good train service between Newbury and Reading
STARTING GRID REF:	SU 602673
CAR PARKING:	At the station
TRANSPORT:	Regular service to Reading
REFRESHMENT:	All services in Reading and frequent pubs alongside the walk
NEAREST TIC:	The Town Hall, Blagrave Street, Reading, Berkshire RG12 1QH - 01734 566226

THE WALK

The town, famous - or was it notorious? - as the destination of the anti-nuclear campaigner marches in the 1950s and '60s, is a pleasant village on the outer limit of the London commuting area, almost unknown until the Atomic Weapons Research Establishment was opened in the early 1950s. There is a car park at the station, and a good train service to Reading.

Leave the station and turn right down Tudor Road to the bottom, turning right again, under the railway, into Caversham Road. At the main junction beyond, turn right and take the first left which is De Montfort Road. At the bottom of this street is the Thames.

Reading to Fobney - 4 miles

Turn right. Pass Caversham lock and View Island where the river sweeps left and then right. After almost a mile, the attractive Horseshoe Bridge crosses the Kennet. Turn right alongside the river, under a railway bridge and

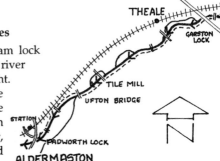

to Blakes lock. Across the water is Blakes Lock Museum. Access is possible from the next bridge at Gasworks Road, and it is well worth the short detour. The attractive buildings used to be part of a pumping station, but are now an exposition of Reading past. Some of the old town's trades are recreated including, for example, a printer, bakery and gentleman's hairdresser. There is a breathtakingly beautiful gypsy caravan built locally by Dunton and Sons, who were famous in their day for this type of work. This section of the walk also follows the Kennet Cycleway.

The canal arrives at a narrow section controlled by traffic signals, and just beyond is Duke Street Bridge. Here the towpath disappears for a short while, and the walk follows roads. Up on the road, turn left and right at the traffic lights. To your left is the elevated inner ring road, to your right, the bus garage. Cross over the next island, and at the far side is a gateway into a car park which gives access to the towpath by County lock. The towpath leaves in a southerly direction on the right-hand bank.

After passing under the ring road, Reading starts to fall behind, and the canal gradually takes on the more peaceful mien that characterises this walk. The last of the factories is marked by a right-

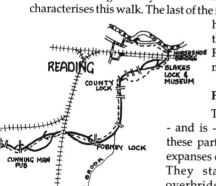

hand bend that shortly fetches the walk up at the next lock, Fobney. Here the towpath moves to the left-hand side.

Fobney to Theale - 3½ miles

That gravel extraction has been - and is - a popular pastime around these parts is witnessed by the huge expanses of water-filled old workings. They start just by the railway overbridge, linking Reading with Basingstoke, and now a busy link between the midland and the north, and the Hampshire coast.

Southcote lock sees Reading making a last despairing effort to impose itself on the canal, but failure is assured as

41

rurality reigns and, after crossing a bridge over the river as it leaves to the south, the Cunning Man pub, canalside at Burgfield Bridge, is reached. This Courage house is very popular locally, and rightly so; pause awhile and enjoy the atmosphere.

The next bridge is of the roving variety, seeing the towpath move to the right-hand bank for a mile or so, past Burgfield lock and back to the left. It was here, in 1720, that riots took place when the canalised section was under construction. Over 300 people, including local business people, worried about the effect of the canal on trade, took things very much into their own hands and wrecked the workings.

Soon the tranquillity is destroyed by the M4 motorway screaming overhead. It must be a pleasant thought to those hardy souls, the long distance walkers, that the next 70 miles of this canal are unaffected by motorways: 88 if you go right to Bristol. There aren't too many other lines that can make a similar claim. Garston lock was originally a turf-sided chamber. The restoration has gone a long way to retaining this unusual form of lock. The first swing bridge of the canal (or last if you're walking the other way) is soon encountered at Theale.

Theale to Aldermaston - 3$^{1/2}$ miles

This next section is particularly attractive. Lush tree growth on the right is counterpointed by water-filled disused gravel workings on the left. There are also plenty of wild hops growing alongside the towpath: pleasantly different. The river runs away again on the far side following its own delightful course, as the walk arrives at Tile Mill, for many years during the restoration the limit of navigation. All that has now changed, of course, with the lock and swing bridge in good order. A short canalised section leads back into the river with water meadows now to the left, and Ufton swing bridge. Here the river leaves to the left for the last time, and the walk crosses the water to pass the now ungated Ufton lock, which used to rise a mere 12 inches.

This is the last section of this gentle stroll along the canalised River Kennet, and how pleasant it has become. Trees and utter peace, only disturbed occasionally by the London to West Country railway which closes very briefly before returning to a more respectable distance. It more or less keeps the Kennet and Avon Canal company for the next 30 miles or so.

Ahead lie Padworth lock and a small flurry of activity. Above is the British Waterways yard, a hire boat company, relocated from Reading in 1994, and a fine Visitor Centre. Offering the usual guides and information, this one outdoes many of the others by offering hot tea and coffee and bottles of fresh milk; very welcome after a long walk.

At Aldermaston lift bridge, turn right, away from the canal, and take the first left. This leads back to the station car park. But before that, a very short diversion is in order. Just beyond the magnificent road bridge is Aldermaston lock. Another intriguing restoration project, this was one of the original turf sided locks, but in the 1760s it was enlarged and a scalloped brick shape tried out. It's an Ancient Monument, all the original features having been copied in this recreation.

The spur just below the lock on the north was cut by the Great Western Railway when they bought the canal. It was created as an interchange sidings. The far end was filled in at the start of the second world war and offices for Great Western Railway staff evacuated from Paddington were located there. Stranges Brewery used to be at the south of the lock. It was sold in 1952 after the death of the only son, and the brewery demolished. The canal company once issued a pamphlet describing Aldermaston wharf as "a place of very considerable export of round and hewed timber, scantling, hoops, brooms etc., as well as malt and flour". Imports included coal from Coventry, groceries and manufactured goods.

WALK 8 - NEWBURY TO HUNGERFORD

For this, the second foray along the Kennet and Avon, the terrain has become somewhat more undulating but, at the same time, has cast off the last suggestions of London commuterland. The story of the canal is told in Walk 7.

BEFORE YOU START

WALK DISTANCE: 9 miles
MAP: OS Landranger Series No 174

START:	Hungerford rail station
PUBLIC TRANSPORT:	National Coaches, Intercity Great Western and Thames Trains serve Newbury. Only the latter extend to Hungerford
STARTING GRID REF:	SU 386672
CAR PARKING:	At the station
TRANSPORT:	Regular Thames Trains service to Newbury
REFRESHMENT:	Vast selections in Newbury, waterside pub in Kintbury, good choice in Hungerford
NEAREST TIC:	The Wharf, Newbury, RG14 5AS - 01635 30267

THE WALK

Leave the station building along the drive, turn left at the end and follow the road into the centre of town. Where the road crosses the river, a path on the left leads towards the canal. But before walking straight through the place with hardly a second look, a little time there is adequately repaid.

Newbury was once a cloth town of some wealth, but in recent years hi-tech has caught on in a big way. With fine rail and road links, it became very much a town of modern England with computing and electronics the growth area. In more recent times, this work has fallen away, leaving something of a vacuum that has yet to be effectively filled. For all this, much of the older heart of Newbury has been preserved, and a walkabout reveals many fine examples of the building trade stretching back for almost 300 years. The row of buildings in which the tourist office is housed is one such example.

Newbury Bridge to Kintbury - 5 miles

The actual path to the water is along the side of a shop, turning left to gain the water's edge. The newly rebuilt towpath here gives an impression of being somewhat precarious, but it is only an impression. These first few yards are actually the canalised River Kennet, but above the Town lock, it is pure canal. Beyond the lock chamber, turn awhile and admire the view over the town, with the

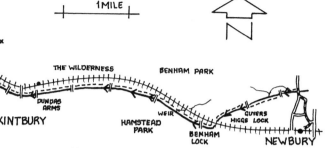

tower of St. Nicholas' church dominating the view. This is a mainly fifteenth century building, and when framed with the surrounding trees has a wonderful visual appeal.

The towpath moves to the left bank over the somewhat dilapidated West Mills swing bridge and, after a short line of moored boats, the canal heads for the outskirts of town, which are soon reached. There is a junction with the river hard by the next bridge, but increasingly now, the walk is alongside the artificial navigation. This is evidenced by the much straighter line of the canal compared with the mainly river section in Walk 7.

The next two locks, Guyers and Higgs, 600 yards along, were named after the opposing commanders of two armies that fought a Civil War battle a couple of miles to the south in 1643. This was the first Battle of Newbury; there was another one a little over a year later to the north of the town. The first one was a bloody affair resulting in a resounding defeat for the forces of the King. They also had to abandon their stronghold in Donnington Castle during the second encounter, although they did take over again a few days later. At Guyers lock the towpath reverts to the right-hand bank.

Water meadows and trees are the order of the day to the right, with the railway line closing from the left before crossing overhead. Benham lock follows, and a little further along is a weir to the right where the Kennet leaves to make its own way to Newbury. Wooded slopes on both sides indicate private parkland; Benham to the right, Hamstead to the left.

The railway is still close, as it will continue to be for the whole of the walk, but there are no roads. The line can be busy at times, carrying the main Paddington to Exeter and the West Country traffic, local services from Great Bedwyn - the westerly limit of Network South East services, and some huge freight trains that snake along the valley looking as though they will never end. Hauled by privately owned US built diesel locomotives, these growling monsters can certainly deliver the power. Those apart, peace is very much the order of the day.

A couple more locks, again in delightfully remote surroundings, leads the towpath into another area of green trees. Known locally as the Wilderness, this is exquisitely beautiful Berkshire and, with virtually no access from a road, not even fishermen get down this section.

This rural idyll lasts for well over a mile before the occasional towpath stroller hoves into view, and moored boats are likely to be seen. The Dundas Arms, on the far bank, presents a pretty face to the water. A bridge and lock end this section.

Kintbury to Hungerford - 4 miles

More moored boats lie above the chamber. Beyond, the river dives away for the last time as the towpath crosses on a pretty bridge. The railway returns to the left-hand side above Brunsden lock. Wire lock follows, and the land to the left becomes much more of a heath,

Relaxing alongside the Kennet and Avon Canal at Hungerford

dotted with trees. This is Hungerford Common which is more closely observed by Dun Hill lock. A few yards to the right the River Kennet is crossed by quite an ordinary bridge, but if the water levels are right, a quick diversion is called for.

Looking over the parapet into the water, there are dozens of ducks congregated at this popular picnic spot. As for fish, there are huge trout inhabiting the area under the bridge. Holding their place in the current, tails moving idly, they are completely unbothered by the ducks, humans splashing in the water close by, or people looking over the bridge. But drop in a piece of bread and watch the water boil.

For this last section the towpath reverts to the left bank. After a rather unkempt open area a bridge is reached. Turn left here to regain the railway station. If you would like to take in the sights of the pretty market town of Hungerford, continue to the next bridge, where the main body of the place is to the left. A road further along on the left will link up with Station Road.

WALK 9 - GREAT BEDWYN TO PEWSEY

This beautifully secluded walk over the summit level of the Kennet and Avon Canal is made very difficult by local public transport. But despite the best efforts of British Rail, it can be done! And be assured that the inconvenience and effort are rewarded with super views, fascinating industrial architecture and continual canal interest.

An arbitrary division is drawn on the rail map of Wiltshire. On the Great Western line from Paddington to Devon and Cornwall, it is decreed that Great Bedwyn shall be the westernmost extent of the Network South East service, the point at which all their services terminate. The next stop on the line westwards is Pewsey. There is no train in either direction booked to stop at both stations. Do not turn to the local bus timetable either: there is no solace or salvation to be found in those pages. But refuse to be beaten.

BEFORE YOU START

WALK DISTANCE: 9 miles
MAP: OS Landranger Sheet 173 & 174

START:	Pewsey rail station
PUBLIC TRANSPORT:	As above
STARTING GRID REF:	SU 161603
CAR PARKING:	At the station
TRANSPORT:	Intercity to Newbury and Network South East return to Great Bedwyn - not Sundays
REFRESHMENT:	Pubs and shops in Great Bedwyn, pub/restaurant halfway, and all services in Pewsey
NEAREST TIC:	George Lane, Marlborough, Wiltshire SN8 1EE - 01672 513989

THE WALK

Catch an eastbound train from Pewsey to Newbury. There, change platforms and connect into the stopping service back to Great Bedwyn. There is a little consolation for having to overshoot the start of the walk so dramatically. Railway and canal follow a largely similar course, and good views are available of a section not covered by the walk. At Great Bedwyn station, leave the train, walk up to the bridge, turn left and cross the canal. There, join the towpath and turn right.

If the village itself appeals, turn right, over the railway, and left at the first junction. Down there are most of the shops, St. Mary's church and Bedwyn Stone Museum. This fascinating display of the stonemason's art is open during normal working hours, having statuary, tombstones and other examples of fine workmanship dating back to the middle of the nineteenth century.

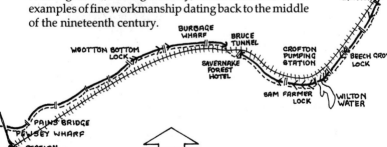

Great Bedwyn to Wilton Top Lock - 3 miles

At once, the atmosphere of this walk is upon you. The gently rolling hills, pretty houses, and a feeling of peace and calm broken only by the occasional passage of a train. The fields on the left look to be a farmer's dream with good loam, but just over a mile away, they will change to a very chalky shallow soil as the hills close in a little. This walk is punctuated by locks: 14 in all, and most on this side of the summit. Ahead is the chimney of Crofton pumping station, to the left, the 8 acres of Wilton Water. This is one of the main reservoirs for the canal's water supply, and is a haven for bird life, particularly duck. In addition to the ubiquitous mallard, teal, pochard and tufted ducks usually in residence, swans, coots and water hen add to the scene.

Unfortunately, this water supply is some 60ft below the summit level, hence the pumping station. Cross the canal and the railway for a look round the place. The building is open to visitors each weekend during the summer, and with occasional "in steam" dates through the season. The chance of seeing the oldest working beam engine in the country doing the job for which it was built is worth planning your walk around. It's fascinating to anyone with even the slightest appreciation of history.

Rescued by the Crofton Society, now a branch of the Kennet and Avon Trust, this pretty building houses two giant steam engines, both in full working order. The original was installed by canal engineer John Rennie in time for the through opening of the canal. The second, a little larger, followed in 1812. They originally pumped from springs until Wilton Water was created in 1836. The first engine was replaced with a new one in 1843, but this never functioned correctly until further work was performed at the turn of the century. By 1958 the upper part of the chimney was removed as unsafe. This created a draughting problem for the boilers, and the steam engines were replaced, initially by a diesel pump, then by an electric one. This pump provides for the day-to-day needs of the canal.

In 1968 the Society purchased Crofton and inaugurated repairs. On 4 April 1970 the 1812 engine moved under its own power. Four months later the then Poet Laureate Sir John Betjeman performed the reopening ceremony. Each one lifts a ton of water at a stroke,

Buildings housing the famed steam-driven beam engines at Crofton on
the Kennet and Avon Canal

depositing it into a leat which runs to an outlet beyond the top lock and makes a magnificent sight. (Information on the society, its activities and "in steam" days is obtainable from the Secretary on 01380 71279.)

The canal now continues its climb. Lock 58 has been named the Sam Farmer lock, after the local agriculturalist and philanthropist. Money from his Trust Fund paid for the restoration of the lock. There is a mass of old brick abutments here where a series of old railway lines used to cross the water heading for Andover (Hants). They came to conquer the canal, succeeded, and in turn succumbed to the roads. Will the twenty-first century see a renaissance of the iron road similar to that of the canals now?

Wilton Top Lock to Wootton Rivers Bottom Lock - 3 miles

To the summit at last. Tree lined, with the beautiful Savernake forest to the north, the canal enters a cutting as it heads for Bruce tunnel. Here the towpath leaves the canal to pass over the top. There is no towpath, and a chain used to be provided for bargees to haul their boats through.

A feature of this canal so far is the wonderfully diverse range of bird life. The usual range of hedgerow and water birds are there in abundance, and woodpeckers hard at work are heard, if not often seen. This cornucopia of feathers, very strangely, virtually ceases to exist beyond the tunnel, a state of affairs for which there seems no rational explanation. The path dips under the railway here and returns to the waterside. Still remote, still very pretty, and very lightly used by the locals, the path reaches Burbage Wharf, with a delightful crane mounted canalside.

This is effectively the start of the Vale of Pewsey and the first of the "downhill" locks at Cadley. Pretty old farmhouses with wonderfully ornate chimney stacks can be seen on both sides of the canal. Wootton Bottom lock is the last of 14 on this walk. They offer the boater a diverse selection of paddle gear to attack, some of it ungeared and clearly designed for Superman.

Wootton Bottom Lock to Pewsey - 3 miles

After passing a collection of moored boats, the canal now crosses a series of undulations by cutting and embankment, the vale to the

Burbage Wharf on the Kennet and Avon Canal

left providing splendid views. Recesses provided for flood gates can be seen at successive bridges, although the gates themselves have gone. Pewsey Wharf is a very attractive end to the walk. There is a tearoom here open during the season, and it also appears a popular spot with local fishermen. Exactly how boaters react to having their mooring space taken over by anglers is probably worth waiting to see: if you can stand the sight of blood!

Leave the canal here. Turn left, and the station is just $^1/_2$ mile along the road which is quite narrow and has no footpath, making care essential.

WALK 10 - SEEND CLEEVE TO DEVIZES

A "must" on any towpath walker's schedule, the Caen Hill flight of locks is arguably the most stunning on the whole system. Sixteen of them in tight formation, each with an acre of side pound, storm up the hill in quite spectacular fashion. This is not a long walk, but the exact distance will be decided by which bus you manage to get back. Again on the Kennet and Avon Canal, transport is a problem.

BEFORE YOU START

WALK DISTANCE:	5 miles
MAP:	OS Landranger Sheet 173
START:	Devizes Wharf Car Park
PUBLIC TRANSPORT:	Nearest railhead, Chippenham or Trowbridge
STARTING GRID REF:	SU 004618
CAR PARKING:	See above
TRANSPORT:	Plenty of variety, but little continuity. One service operates on the 3rd Saturday of every month! Badgerline Service 272, Devizes to Bath, calls at the end of Seend Cleeve Lane, about ¹/₂ mile from the canal. The Seend Shuttle operates infrequently from Devizes to the Barge, or Badgerline Service 77 runs to Trowbridge along the A361, calling at Seend Cleeve, about ¹/₂ mile from the canal. The whole is co-ordinated by Wiltshire Bus - 01345 090899
REFRESHMENT:	Full range in Devizes, pub at far end, further pubs towards end of walk
NEAREST TIC:	39 St. Johns Street, Devizes, Wiltshire SN10 1BL - 01380 729408

THE WALK

Walk away from the canal into Couch Lane and cross the main road into Snuff Street. This leads into a large square, Market Cross. The bus stops are scattered around the square, but tend to leave from the far side. If you are on the Melksham service, alight at the end of Seend Cleeve Lane which is on the left. Walk down here for some

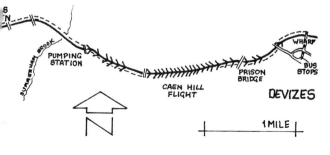

500 yards and take the right turn which soon after reaches the canal bridge: turn left along the towpath.

Arriving along the Trowbridge road, alight at the top of Seend Lane, near Great Thornham Farm. Cross the road and walk down through the village of Seend Cleeve to the canal. Cross the bridge and turn right.

If you are fortunate enough to get a service into the village, ask for the nearest stop to the Barge.

Seend Cleeve to Devizes Bottom Lock - 2½ miles

At Seend Cleeve Wharf the towpath heads east towards Devizes and the first of 32 locks that punctuate progress, and see the finish nearly 260ft higher than the start. Strange though it may appear today, there was an ironworks here until the start of this century, but finding any trace is not easy.

The going is good with a fine firm towpath, a condition which obtains throughout the walk. The view now is pastoral, rural Wiltshire at its finest. Just over ½ mile into the walk, having passed two other locks in the Seend flight, is the second swing bridge and

To eliminate water shortage on the Devizes lock flight, a back-pumping scheme was constructed in 1995. A plaque records the event on the pump house at Lower Foxhanger, Kennet and Avon Canal

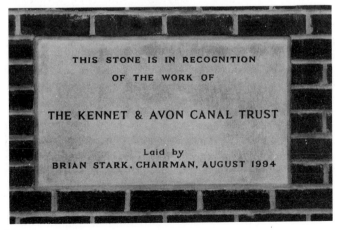

54

the site of an old coal wharf. Sells Green is on the left, a pretty little village with an excellent pub, the Three Magpies, just up the lane on the main road. An undistinguished aqueduct over Summerham Brook keeps the line moving eastward, but there is nothing very exciting for the next mile or so.

But this is only the calm before the metaphorical storm. Already, the town of Devizes can be picked out on top of the hill, and the first of the Devizes flight of locks arrives. A new building over the other side of the water is a new pumping station. Water is very scarce on this flight, and a massive fund-raising operation is still under way. This pump returns water used in the locking process, 70,000 gallons for each lock, to the top.

Devizes Bottom Lock to Devizes Wharf - 2½ miles

The towpath changes sides over a rustic brick bridge at the tail of the bottom lock. There are now six chambers fairly evenly spaced, until the next road bridge. There is one lock immediately after the bridge and then the Caen Hill flight starts in earnest. Admire the house just to the right. Once owned by the Kennet and Avon Company, it was provided for the canal engineer, but was eventually sold and turned into a laundry which drained waste water into the canal, making a very soapy pound. It is now privately owned.

Construction of the Caen Hill flight caused a long delay in the through opening of the canal. Boats could use the section to the west by 1801, but it was not until 28 December 1810 that work here was completed and the through link finished. From 1804, in an effort to keep traffic moving, a horse drawn tramway was provided to by-pass the flight, freight being transshipped at the top and bottom. It was only fitting that when the whole canal was reopened in 1990, Her Majesty The Queen should perform the ceremony at these locks.

The next thousand yards or so provides that rarity on Canal walks: an uphill section. This wonderful flight of locks are so close together that there is hardly a respite in the slope. But unless your legs really aren't up to it, please don't be tempted to walk it downhill. Appreciation of the drama of this flight will be much attenuated if you do.

Soon, the locks start to collect names; those of various worthies without whose efforts the canal would undoubtedly still be unopened for boats. The limited boat movements of today are a considerable change from the days when gas lighting was installed on the flight to allow night working. Any movement after dark collected an extra 1 shilling (5p) charge. This was to help defray the cost of gas used: supplied by the Company, of course.

The main road passes noisily overhead by lock 47 at Prison Bridge. There was actually a prison here, but demolition took place many years ago. The Black Horse pub is on the non-towpath side if refreshment is needed. Inevitably, they sell Wadworth's beer. After another road overbridge the top lock is reached and the towpath changes to the left bank. Here, the steamy sweet smell of a brewery should be evident. It's across the way just above the top lock, backing onto the canal. Wadworth's has a fine (and justified) reputation locally, and most of the town's pubs seem to sell it.

This section of canal is the start of what is known as the Long Pound: 15 miles from here to the next flight of four locks at Wootton Rivers and the summit pound - see Walk 7. The canal has now lifted to well over 450ft above sea level. At the next bridge, cross and return to the Wharf.

Before you leave the waterside, spend a little time at Devizes Wharf. Handsomely restored, two of the original buildings still stand. One has been converted into a theatre. But perhaps one of the finest buildings on the canal is the old granary. Built in 1810, it is now occupied by the Kennet and Avon Canal Trust. They have a fine exhibition, a shop, and offer the chance to join them in their good works, or make a contribution to the Water Appeal.

WALK 11 - BATH TO AVONCLIFF or BRADFORD-ON-AVON

Georgian grandeur and pleasant wooded hillsides dominate this walk in what used to be Somerset: and may well be again should the county of Avon be dismantled. The Kennet and Avon Canal offers the walker a good towpath for the whole of this walk, but with one warning: it is also a popular route for cyclists.

BEFORE YOU START

WALK DISTANCE:	8¹/₂ or 10 miles
MAP:	OS Landranger Sheets 172 and 173
START:	Avoncliff or Bradford-on-Avon rail station
PUBLIC TRANSPORT:	As above
STARTING GRID REF:	ST 825606 or ST 805601
CAR PARKING:	Side street at Avoncliff, station car park at Bradford
TRANSPORT:	Good train service to Bath
REFRESHMENT:	Everything at Bradford, tearoom at Avoncliff just before the aqueduct, tearoom and pub at Bathhampton, everything you can imagine in Bath
NEAREST TIC:	The Library, Bridge Street, Bradford-on-Avon, Wiltshire BA15 1BY - 01225 865797
	The Colonnades, 11-13 Bath Street, Bath, Avon BA1 1SW - 01225 462831

THE WALK

Catch the train at your chosen station and alight at Bath. Leave the building, turn right and immediately on the right are two arches marked No Entry To Vehicles. Walk under these and cross the footbridge which takes you over the River Avon.

Bath to Bathampton - 2¹/₂ miles

At the far end turn left into Claverton Street which leads after 100 yards to Widcombe lock, the actual start of the Kennet and Avon Canal. A plaque attached to the wall of the Thimble Mill, a wine bar and public house, commemorates the restoration of the flight from 1969 to 1976, at the expense of the Kennet and Avon Canal Trust and the City of Bath.

It is always a wise move to allow extra time to enjoy the glories of this wonderful city, a showpiece for the finest in Georgian architecture. Some of the most talented designers in our history have displayed their aesthetic skills here: John Wood, his son, Robert Adam and Thomas Baldwin have all left their mark on this extraordinary city.

Turn left before the locks and follow the Avon for a couple of hundred yards; it is possible to see one of Robert Adam's glorious works. Pulteney Bridge is Classical architecture at its finest. Follow the flight of steps up to the road and admire the shops that line the bridge. Look over towards Grand Parade across the water. There is the Guildhall, and church spires everywhere: a classic city.

Almost reluctantly, to business. Immediately beyond the bottom lock are a couple of road overbridges, and the towpath leads to a deep concrete cavern of a lock; not an original. It's an amalgamation of two chambers occasioned by the need to expand Pulteney Road, the A36, to meet modern traffic requirements. That action has produced the deepest chamber in the country with an $18^{1}/_{2}$ft fall: or rise, walking in this direction. Here, the towpath changes to the left-hand bank.

Just before the fourth chamber, on the left, a gap in the housing reveals how high the towpath has already climbed above the city; a magnificent view over the rooftops with the abbey towers prominent. Local stone, used in virtually every building, creates a very pleasant effect from up here, even if the original white has turned a creamy-grey over the years.

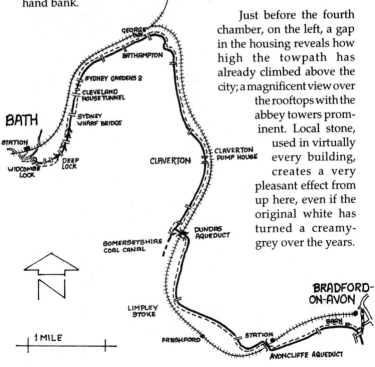

Pretty canalside cottages at Bathampton on the Kennet and Avon Canal

Beyond the top lock, houses and trees start to recede for a while. There are more views over Bath and beyond until reaching the next bridge, which is of the turnover variety. Up the steps, cross the road to regain the towpath on the right. Opposite is Sydney Wharf, once an integral part of the trade along this line. Currently it is the base for a boatyard. Now the city disappears completely as the towpath goes into an oasis of peace - apart from the traffic sounds. This is the start of Sydney Gardens, and the location of Cleveland House, once the headquarters of the Kennet and Avon company.

This fine building is constructed directly over the canal, and the towpath, as it returns to the left bank, passes the front door. A short tunnel leads into more beauty, with a couple of very attractive cast iron bridges sitting on stone abutments. These carry a plaque indicating that they were erected in Anno 1800. Another short tunnel, Sydney Gardens No. 2, has an ornate bas-relief figure carved over the entrance.

The next building towpath-side is rather odd shaped with walls sloping inwards, and inscribed with the legend "Bath Humane Society's Station for Lifebuoys and Dragpoles". They also offer a reward of 5 shillings (25p) "...for anyone giving such information as will lead to the conviction of any persons found damaging or removing this apparatus or using it for any other purpose than that for which it is supplied".

The canal makes a sharp right turn now, with yet more splendid views across to the left over the outskirts of Bath and the Avon valley. The railway is just over the wall on what was once the canal's bed. When the railway arrived, an Act of Parliament was passed to allow the rerouting of the canal to accommodate their tracks, a mere 30 years after the original line was cut. The canal travels almost due east now for well over a mile. A collection of boats moors along here.

Bathampton to Dundas - 3 miles

At Bathampton Bridge, the attractive George Inn offers Courage beer. The inn is extremely old, and was once part of a priory. The local school and the parish church of St. Nicholas are next-door, whilst across the water, the large garden is inhabited by a huge collection of the most outlandish gnomes you could ever hope to see!

The valley makes another right turn, taking canal and river with it, and heads due south for a while. Canal Farm, located right on the bend, is a very pleasant building with a sun dial on its wall. Bridges along this section are few and far between and come in many guises; including the ubiquitous swing bridge. In the valley to the left, which is narrowing considerably, the river and railway close in, with the beautiful Warley Manor on the far side, covered in the most enchanting maroon Virginia Creeper.

Just before Claverton Bridge, a road leads down to Claverton Pumping Station which supplies the canal with water from the Avon. Designed by John Rennie, its two undershot wheels provided pumping power until 1952 when it was replaced by a diesel. Now restored by the Kennet and Avon Trust, it performs its original function on certain "Pumping Weekends". It's open every Sunday from April to September, with details of pumping days available on 01225 462831. For day to day operation, British Waterways use electricity.

Across the bridge and up the road is Claverton itself. A straggly settlement alongside the A36, St. Mary the Virgin's churchyard holds the mortal remains of Ralph Allen, one of the creators of

*A very attractive pub to be found canalside at Bathampton,
Kennet and Avon Canal*

Georgian Bath. There is also a Manor House which contains a Museum of American Life. This exposition of America between the seventeenth and nineteenth centuries is a fascinating display of the many facets of early days in the new world.

The next fixed bridge, a quite ugly iron structure about a mile along, takes the towpath to the right bank, and the entrance to the Somersetshire Coal Canal. Opened in 1801 as a narrow beam canal, it served the Somerset coalfield - yes, there really was one: 165,000 tons was shipped along the canal in 1858. Caisson locks, inclined planes and conventional locks were all tried in an attempt to smooth out the hilly terrain, but these problems, and the arrival of the railway by mid century, saw the whole thing fall into disuse, finally closing in 1898. All that remains is about 500 yards, now used for moorings and as a hire boat base.

Dundas to Avoncliffe - 3 miles

Crossing the lift bridge over the entrance to the Somersetshire Coal Canal, what was the site of an old stop lock can be seen. Immediately ahead is another superb structure: Dundas Aqueduct. This takes the canal over the Avon and the railway, to the far side of the valley. As with most aqueducts, it is difficult to appreciate its majesty from the towpath. At the far end, steps lead into the field below to give the chance to see its full glory.

The canal now becomes very tree lined, changing the character completely. It is wide, but the whole still manages to retain an intimacy that lasts to Limpley Stoke Bridge. As the canal continues its course around a sharp left-hand bend with bosky hillside across the water and only an occasional dwelling, it really is most picturesque. At the end of this length, a sharp right takes that canal over Avoncliffe Aqueduct.

For those leaving the walk here, the station is virtually underneath the aqueduct. Follow the signposted way to the station car park beyond.

Avoncliffe to Bradford-on-Avon - 1¹/₂ miles

A sharp left turn past some quite attractive housing, and the canal is away into isolation again. Along here, it runs in what appears to be a trough. Historically, this section was always very prone to leaks. After restoration revealed the continuation of this problem, British Waterways, using modern techniques, spent £0.8m in 1990 to properly waterproof the bed.

Approaching the road bridge in Bradford, the towpath leaves the waterside close to a tearoom and pub. On reaching the road, turn left and the station is a short walk down this road.

Chapter 3:
Buckinghamshire, Oxfordshire and Northamptonshire

WALK 12 - MARSWORTH TO AYLESBURY - AYLESBURY ARM, GRAND UNION CANAL

Only an hour's drive from the metropolis, this 6$^{1/2}$ mile walk along the northern slope of the Chilterns and down into the Vale of Aylesbury is beautifully rural, only skirting the village of Wilstone between the start and finish. This is the area of the Chiltern Hundreds. The name incidentally, is applied to Crown lands, and was once an administrative division supposed to contain 100 families or freemen.

The canal was originally envisaged as a link between the Grand Union and Abingdon, on the River Thames near Oxford. The aim was to provide a through link to the Wiltshire and Berkshire and the Thames and Severn canals. In the event, only this part of it was ever built, vehement opposition from local landowners being the main cause of the abandonment of plans.

The Aylesbury Arm (as it eventually became known) was opened in 1814 as a branch from the Grand Junction's line from London to Braunston. The junction was actually made at Startops End, although the name of the larger adjacent village of Marsworth was adopted. But that nomenclature was seldom applied by the old boatmen; it was soon corrupted to "Maffers", a name still used to this day.

From there, the line dropped through 16 narrow locks, the most southerly narrow ones on the canal system, into Aylesbury, where a huge collection of buildings and warehouses was built. Early trade tended to be building materials in and farm produce out. Factories were attracted to the waterside, and one, the Aylesbury Condensed Milk Company, survives to this day under the Nestlé banner. One of the more famed canal carriers, Harvey Taylor Ltd, was based in the town.

Trade rapidly fell away in this century and, as with so many other canals, the formation of a Canal Society was instrumental in saving the line from the near dereliction into which it had fallen.

BEFORE YOU START

WALK DISTANCE:	6¹/₂ miles
MAP:	OS Landranger Sheet 165
START:	Walton Street, Aylesbury. This is the A413 Wendover road
PUBLIC TRANSPORT:	Chiltern Lines trains from London Marylebone to Aylesbury
STARTING GRID REF:	SP 822135
CAR PARKING:	Walton Street, Aylesbury
TRANSPORT:	Luton & District service 61 to Luton. Service details on 01296 84919
REFRESHMENT:	Pubs at "Maffers", all services at Aylesbury
NEAREST TIC:	8 Bourbon Street, Aylesbury, Buckinghamshire HP20 2RR - 01296 330559

THE WALK

Walk down Walton Street and turn right into Exchange Street from where the bus departs. Alight at the White Lion, Marsworth. Cross the canal bridge and turn left onto the towpath. Or perhaps a stroll across the road to the vast Startops End (or Tringford) reservoir. Here, hides are provided to allow observation of the wide range of birds finding a home here. It is also on migratory routes, and at the appropriate times, several unusual species can be seen. Marsworth reservoir adjoins this one, and both supply water to the canal.

Marsworth to Redhouse Lock - 3 miles

This is actually the Grand Union main line, but only remains

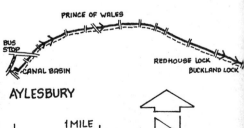

Pulteney Bridge, Bath (Walk 11)
The Kennet & Avon Canal near Freshford (Walk 11)

Aylesbury arm of the Grand Union Canal (Walk 12)
The canal at Oxford (Walk 16)

so for a hundred yards. During that time, the junction on the left, many moored boats and the British Waterways yard are all passed. There is no crossing to the branch, so leave the canal at the next road bridge, turn left, walk to the next bridge and turn left again to reach the junction.

Over the canal in Marsworth, the thirteenth-century squat square tower of All Saints church stands out above all else. It was largely rebuilt in the last century, and is home to a splendid painting of a pregnant Virgin Mary by Jan Pienkowski. It was given by the artist in 1989, and local children have provided additional decoration to the edge.

Having examined the staircase lock, it is time to turn round. The Plain of Aylesbury lies ahead, fields with their different hues adding a delectable patchwork effect to the view, with the destination hidden in the summer haze - or winter mists!

After the first lock below the road bridge, there appears an anomaly of local government. Although there is nothing to indicate it, the county line between Buckinghamshire and Hertfordshire is here. The latter extends a 2 mile wide finger some several miles into Buckinghamshire at this point, for no apparent reason.

Locks come thick and fast in this length, and before long, the edge of Wilstone is reached. At bridge 3, $^1/_4$ mile to the left is the Half Moon pub, an excellent place serving Aylesbury Brewery Company's beers. There is also a shop and post office close by.

And it's time to play the Crazy County game again. Back into Buckinghamshire at lock 10, out again below bridge 7, some 250 yards on, returning for the last time after another $^1/_2$ mile just before bridge 8. There must be a sound reason for this erratic line that is not attributable to intoxicated surveyors!

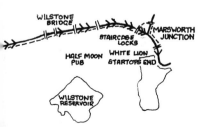

Redhouse Lock to Aylesbury Basin - 3½ miles

The walk continues through the most delightfully bucolic scenery, maintaining this until Aylesbury finally begins to makes its presence felt. The last lock, set amid overhanging willow trees, is thoroughly picturesque. The Nestlé factory is passed, advertising Campbell and Maggi, two of their acquired brand names.

A prettily rebuilt bridge gives access to the basin area, crammed with boats, many of them traditional working boats, some having been converted for living aboard, with variable results. The basin is also home to as diverse a variety of ducks as can be seen anywhere on the canal network: shelduck, widgeon, pochard, merganser and little grebe in addition to the ubiquitous mallard and waterhen. There are also a couple of varieties of geese. Locals say that they are always to be seen, well fed by resident and boater alike. The one breed that is noticeable by its absence is the Aylesbury duck!

The towpath now reaches the water's end, and bears round to the right. Follow this path under the canopy of a new building, and round to the road. This is Walton Street, by the Ship Inn, a Benskin's house.

If you still have the energy, the town itself makes a pleasant exploration. A free booklet detailing the Aylesbury Town Trail gives a fascinating insight into the town: it's only a mile and is well worth the time and effort as you discover the architectural pearls that lie well hidden hereabouts. The TIC and library have copies.

WALK 13 - BERKHAMSTED TO HEMEL HEMPSTEAD - GRAND UNION CANAL

A pleasant stroll that offers the opportunity for expansion into something longer if required. It is also along the main line of the Grand Junction Canal, now the Grand Union.

The Grand Union Canal was formed as recently as 1929, an amalgamation of all the canals between London and Birmingham with many smaller branches. But by far the major component was the Grand Junction Company. This had started life building the line between the Thames at Brentford and Braunston.

Braunston was once the hub of long distance canal carrying in England. This was where the Grand Junction joined the Oxford. Coal carrying boats from the Warwickshire coalfield met the manufacturing cargoes travelling to and from Birmingham.

A major achievement in its day, the canal was the first north/south canal that had to cross two watersheds in its 93 mile run. The long climb out of London over the Chilterns, part of which is covered during this walk, was followed by a descent into the Ouse valley. Then a climb to Buckby before plunging down again en route to the Avon valley.

It was constructed as a barge canal (14ft wide locks), and built to a very high standard. As the main transport artery between England's capital and the second city, it was a very busy line, actually carrying regular freight until 1969. This was coal, travelling along the northern section of the Oxford to Braunston and then down to a factory on the outskirts of London.

After the amalgamation in 1929, a major upgrading was undertaken with government money in an attempt to secure freight along the Grand Union. The northern section - from Napton to Birmingham - had been built with 7ft locks. These were rebuilt as barge locks, with major dredging and bank protection works adding to the improvements.

But to no avail. Before any real benefits could be seen, the war started. Plans to replace narrowboats with barges and widen the Leicester Arm were stillborn. With it went the last hope that inland waterway carrying could be sustained, and the trend from 1945 onwards was one of ever reducing trade.

This was exacerbated by nationalisation in 1948. The British Transport Commission, charged with operating all surface transport, clearly saw the canals as obsolete and an aggressive programme of transferring freight to their rail and road services started. Canals were even more neglected than they had been prior to the war and many lost their trade during this period, including some of the Grand Union branches.

With small independent carriers starting business on the Grand Union in an attempt to keep some freight, this main line was never seriously threatened with closure. Enthusiasts-cum-businessmen made valiant attempts against the odds to keep trade on the water, but with coal usage, the staple cargo, dwindling, it was a vain struggle in one respect, though their actions ensured that the goods carrying and leisure ages overlapped, and the Grand Union moved seamlessly between the two.

Grand Union towpaths have come in for much improvement in recent years. They were allowed to decay after the demise of horse drawn boats, and several lengths were impassable for years. Then, conscious of the rapid increase in towpath walking, British Waterways started working with local councils to reinstate them. Now we have a high profile long distance footpath between London and Birmingham. This 145 mile walk was opened, to great acclaim, in 1993 to the benefit of everyone from the ten minute stroller before a pub visit through to the dedicated walker, many of whom do walk the whole length.

BEFORE YOU START

WALK DISTANCE:	4 miles
MAP:	OS Landranger Series Nos 165 & 166
START:	Hemel Hempstead rail station
PUBLIC TRANSPORT:	Trains and coaches serve the town
STARTING GRID REF:	TQ 042059
CAR PARKING:	Station (pay)
TRANSPORT:	North London Railways, regular service including Sundays
REFRESHMENT:	Both ends, one pub en route
NEAREST TIC:	Dacorum Information Centre, Marlowes, Hemel Hempstead, Hertfordshire - 01442 60161

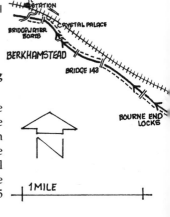

Berkhamsted to Winkwell Swing Bridge - 2½ miles

On arrival at Berkhamsted station, there is a decision to be reached. To start the walk at once, leave the platform down the steps and turn right. Cross the forecourt and the road. At the canal turn left. The towpath is on the far side here, but on reaching the first bridge, 75 yards away, returns to the left bank. Join it, and walk under the bridge.

The short alternative diversion takes in Berkhamsted Castle. To reach it, turn left at the bottom of the stairs and leave the station through the east exit. Turn right, cross the road, keeping the railway close to the right, and walk up the road opposite for a few yards. The entrance to this English Heritage site is a few yards along. To pick up the walk again, leave the site, turn right and first left under the railway. The canal is across the road from there; follow the directions as above.

Berkhamsted Castle is typical of the motte and bailey type of construction that was popular immediately after the Norman invasion. The motte was a circular earth mound on which a tower was built, the bailey being the outer area that was enclosed by some form of wall or fence that could be defended. This particular example was robustly built from flint and stone. There is still much remaining, and the carefully tended grounds are usually open. Entered in the visitor book - were there such a thing - would have been the names of Geoffrey Chaucer, Thomas à Becket, and the young Henry Tudor with his court. The castle had fallen into ruin by 1495, and much of the materials used in its construction were recycled to build houses in the town.

Berkhamsted has long been a prosperous town. In the Middle Ages, its wealth came from wool. There has been a high quality public school in the town for hundreds of years, the original (Tudor) buildings dating from 1541. One famous alumnus was the author Graham Greene. Today, it is essentially a commuter town, although it retains a very strong sense of its own identity.

Immediately under the bridge across the water is a very unexpected sight: a North American Indian totem pole. It's genuine, too. The site was used for many years by a timber merchant whose parent company was in Canada. They sent it across for display in 1967. All was fine until the company decided to move. There was a plan for the totem to move as well, so the local council slapped a preservation order on it: and there it

WINKWELL LOCKS

SWING BRIDGE

THREE HORSESHOES

BOXMOOR LOCK

FISHERY LOCK

STATION

stands, incongruous, not exactly pretty, but compellingly interesting.

On the left is a milepost, indicating that it is 61 miles to Braunston. This is a replacement, the original having disappeared. Over recent years the Canal Society have made great efforts to replace those that were missing, and have now succeeded. The names of any sponsors are cast in the base plate.

The first of several pubs is now discovered. The Crystal Palace is not quite as grand as its name suggests, but has tables directly alongside the towpath. Across the way is the hire base of Bridgewater Boats. This company was founded in the 1970s by Mike and Lindy Foster. Over the years, Lindy has become a doughty campaigner for the waterways and their environment.

The Boat Inn will be found by Berkhamsted lock. This is a Fullers house. And, in case you get thirsty quickly, the Rising Sun will be found by the next lock. It sells Benskins, and has given its name to the lock.

A short section of attractive canal follows, only partly marred by the presence of a factory on the far bank, and, as bridge 143 is reached, the towpath moves to the right-hand side. Berkhamsted is left behind, but the views never become expansive as the line closely follows the valley of the River Bulbourne. The original A41 trunk road - now thankfully further away on a by-pass - and the busy railway line also share this valley. The road intrudes very little; the railway is always within earshot if not actual sight.

Lock chambers occur at regular intervals until a rather attractive electrically controlled swing bridge is reached.

Winkwell Swing Bridge to Fishery Inn - 1½ miles

Across the bridge is the setting for a fine pub, the Three Horseshoes. There has been a pub here since 1535, and the range of beers on offer is wide. Food is also served.

High overhead, the railway crosses the water on a fine brick viaduct and the canal, having weaved under it, assumes a relatively straight line for the remainder of this walk.

Boats moored on the left-hand side and the approach of a lock indicate the end of this walk. Leave the towpath, noting that the recently refurbished Fishery Inn is just over the bridge, if required, and turn right along Fishery Road. At the end, cross the road and Hemel Hempstead station is directly opposite.

WALK 14 - BUCKLAND WHARF TO COWROAST - GRAND UNION CANAL & WENDOVER BRANCH

Most of the lines making up the Grand Union Canal survived into the leisure age, just a few short branches succumbing. They have all now been infilled, except the Wendover Branch.

This was opened in 1797, primarily to act as a water feed from springs in the Chiltern Hills to the main Grand Junction Canal then under construction. It was $^3/_4$ miles long, running from the main line just above Marsworth Top lock to the eponymous town. It was constructed as a narrow canal - the main line was "broad" - and fed water to the main system for many years.

A badly puddled bed was the source of continual leaks, and to that end a stop lock at Tringford was installed. To no avail. A defective canal bed midway along the branch was actually leaking more water out than the pumps were providing, so all but the first $1^1/_2$ miles were closed in 1904. The section from Tringford to

Traditional carrying narrowboats at Bulbourne on the Grand Union Canal. Lock gates for the south of England are manufactured in the buildings across the water

Drayton Beauchamp was drained.

With the arrival of the leisure age, a society was formed to promote restoration of the whole length. To this end, much clearance work was carried out by volunteers, British Waterways and Manpower Services during the 1980s.

Now, all the towpath is walkable, and there are firm proposals to rewater the whole length. There are several major stumbling blocks to this work, but, with the power of the restoration movement today, everything is possible.

BEFORE YOU START

WALK DISTANCE:	7 miles
MAP:	OS Landranger Series No 165
START:	Cowroast. This is a few yards to the east of the old A41 London to Aylesbury road north-west of Berkhamsted. The new by-pass now avoids the place
PUBLIC TRANSPORT:	Berkhamsted and Tring both have good rail services
STARTING GRID REF:	SU 958103
CAR PARKING:	A few spaces roadside, or at the pub (with permission)
TRANSPORT:	Services 501, Hemel Hempstead to Aylesbury, is operated by Red Rose Travel - 01296 399500. Full local service details of TravelLine - 0345 382000
REFRESHMENT:	Pub at Cowroast, one en route, and nothing else
NEAREST TIC:	8 Bourbon Street, Aylesbury, Buckinghamshire HP20 2RR - 01296 330559

THE WALK

Walk the few yards back to the main road, cross opposite the Cowroast Inn, and the bus stop is a few yards along to the right. Alight at Buckland Wharf, where the main road crosses the canal. As a reference point, the main A4011 turns left soon after the bus has rejoined the main road. The wharf is next stop, some 75 yards beyond.

Turn back and cross the road, aiming for a large building with the name "Homesitters" emblazoned on the wall. Here, a public footpath leads away to the left along the towpath.

Buckland Wharf to Tringford Pump - 2½ miles

Immediately, the clarity, shallowness and speed of flow of the water are apparent. Also stunningly obvious - if walked at the correct time of year - is that this first length is a haven for butterflies and moths; enough to have any practising lepidopterist in paroxysms of rapture. Even to the uncultured eye of this writer, the path was alive with red admiral, marbled white, small blue, small tortoiseshell and meadow brown. Quite a picture.

After some 300 yards the flowing canal starts to slacken as it approaches an ugly concrete structure in the bed of the canal. The water disappears into it, and does not come out the other side. From here, the line is quite dry. At the next accommodation bridge, the path turns left and climbs the bank, to continue alongside the course. There is then a meeting of the ways as two paths arrive, one from the left and one from the right.

From here, valiant efforts have been and are being made to

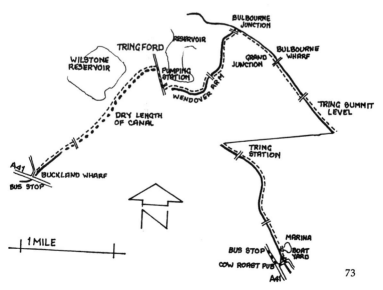

control the growth of bushes and trees in the canal bed, but eventually Mother Nature wins, and the whole basin that contained the water vanishes under green leaves. The towpath also deteriorates quite alarmingly. It is deeply rutted and either bone-crackingly hard or ankle deep in mud - depending on recent weather.

The towpath then reaches a stile. Here the almost indistinguishable bed of the canal snakes off to the right. The path continues to a narrow country lane; turn right. Shortly, the entrance to Tringford Pumping Station is passed on the left, followed by houses that comprise Little Tring as the road starts uphill. On reaching the brow, a white fence indicates the canal bridge. Looking to the right, it is possible to identify the course by the hedge still growing. Turn half left, down to the towpath. For the first 100 yards or so there is very little to distinguish it from what has gone before. But then: water.

Tringford Pump to Bulbourne Junction - 1¹/₂ miles

Take the path to the left-hand side of the water, past the pumping station. Pass through a gate and walk alongside the now navigable canal. After ¹/₂ mile factory buildings on the right indicate activity. This is Heygate's Flour Mill, once users of the canal for the carriage of freight. Now it all moves in huge lorries that growl around the narrow lanes hereabouts.

The towpath moves to the right bank again for the last section on the Wendover Branch, and soon arrives at a bridge which takes the main line towpath over the branch. Turn right.

Bulbourne Junction to Cowroast Lock - 2 miles

As Marsworth Top lock is just to the left, this walk will now cover the full length of the summit pound. Around the corner, picnic tables and barbecues are to be found. Across the water are the workshops of British Waterways. Here, every lock gate in the south of England is manufactured. There are always new examples, often over the edge of the wharf, being kept wet prior to installation.

The Grand Junction pub - serving Greenalls beers - is on the left, with access from the towpath happily restored after one recent landlord closed it. A road bridge passes overhead, and Tring Cutting commences. This took no less than five years to dig. It's wide, peaceful, tree lined and very pretty. Kingfishers live here, and it is often possible to see the flash of electric blue low down to the water as one makes a hasty exit.

It is also an area of intelligent fish: or so it seems. They can clearly read the sign that allows no fishing from the lock to the pub, congregating in that area. On a warm day, carp beyond count will bask near the surface, some real monsters amongst them, rolling languidly. Beyond the bridge, po-faced fishermen sit, waiting for the occasional tiddler to bite.

At the next bridge the towpath will cross to the left bank and get quite narrow as the cutting side, overgrown with bushes, tries to reclaim the territory.

One curio to be discovered on this length is a horse-ramp. This is a gap in the towpath edge with a slope leading down into the water. If a towing horse fell into a canal with built-up edges, it could not climb back out. It was then led to a spot such as this. They are not common on the Grand Union but can be frequently seen on the Leeds and Liverpool Canal.

A final curiosity can be noted in the garden of the lock house at Cowroast on the left: a small lined pond, well stocked with terrapin, growing to quite a considerable size.

At the lock is another pumping station. This pumps water that has been used by the lock back into the top pound. From here the Grand Union starts its plunge to the River Thames, some 60 locks and 36 miles away.

On the hills to the left approaching Cowroast lock is the Ashridge Estate, now owned by the National Trust. This covers some 6 square miles and 4,000 acres of common land, downland and woodland. Deer roam freely in this glorious area. Atop the hill is a 108ft high column, erected in 1832 to commemorate the Duke of Bridgewater, father of Inland Navigation. There are steps up the inside, leading to a platform which offers commanding views. It is open from April to the end of October every afternoon except Friday.

WALK 15 - WOLVERTON TO NEWPORT PAGNELL - GRAND UNION CANAL

A shortish walk in the Greater Milton Keynes area. The return

Grafton Street aqueduct, built in 1991; Grand Union Canal

transport winds its way through this sprawling conurbation, but the walk stays generally clear of civilisation. It also explores the remains of a canal closed a century and a quarter ago, and, to finish, uses a short section of disused railway track. Then, as extras, there are several optional detours en route, adding further dimensions to this already interesting walk.

A look at the history of the Grand Union Canal can be found in Walk 13. The Newport Pagnell Branch was opened in 1814. There were once marble quarries in this area, and this canal branch carried traffic from them. Coal was the main cargo into the area. There were seven locks in its $1^{1}/_{4}$ mile length, and it survived only until 1864, just before the railway was opened. In fact, much of the railway was built on the canal bed. Newport Pagnell Basin and Public Wharf was actually under the railway station. This has, in turn, disappeared under new building referred to in the text.

BEFORE YOU START

WALK DISTANCE: 6 miles

MAP: OS Landranger Series No 152

START:	Newport Pagnell long stay car park
PUBLIC TRANSPORT:	North London Railways service from Euston to Northampton call at Wolverton. The walk passes this station, so it is possible to pick it up here
STARTING GRID REF:	SP 876439
CAR PARKING:	Several car parks in town. One behind the church is free
TRANSPORT:	CitiBus or Buffalo Travel operate service no. 2 every day of the week
REFRESHMENT:	Pub at the start and two en route. All services in Newport Pagnell
NEAREST TIC:	411 Secklow Gate East, The Food Hall, Milton Keynes, Buckinghamshire MK9 3NE - 01908 232525

THE WALK

Alight at the nearest stop to the roundabout on the A4111 V5 Great Monks Street, opposite Old Wolverton Road where the bus turns right for Wolverton. The official stop is 200 yards before this roundabout, but the bus drivers seem very helpful in these parts, and will often drop you at the very point.

Walk down Old Wolverton Road, past the Galleon Inn, and cross the canal bridge. The towpath entrance is on the left. Walk down to waterside and turn right.

Galleon Inn to Wolverton - 2 miles

Yes, turn right. Before setting out for Newport Pagnell, there is a small detour. On the right are some 74 acres reserved as a wildlife conservation area, and containing a medieval village. Also, looking behind the pub, it is possible to see the remains of a motte and bailey castle.

The canal and path are on an embankment here, and fairly straight. Ten minutes' walk and the valley of the Great Ouse is reached. The canal strides across the gap on a rather splendid aqueduct. Here was a source of much grief for the canal's builders and shareholders alike. The first method of crossing was by locks: four down on the south side, five beyond, climbing out. These took the canal into the river. In times of flood, delays were encountered, and to eliminate this problem an aqueduct was built. It collapsed in 1808 and, after a temporary one, the cast iron replacement was erected in 1811.

Turn around and walk back, past the Galleon Inn. The towpath enters a cutting briefly. On the right are extensive railway carriage repair works. These repaired and rebuilt all the London and North Western Railway - later LMS Railway and BR - rolling stock. Although but a pale shadow of what was once here, it still carries out the original function. Ownership of these, and other similar facilities, changes with bewildering rapidity. Its current title almost depends on the day this walk is used!

Wolverton to Great Linford - 2½ miles

Bridge 71, hard by Wolverton railway station, has a flight of wooden steps up to the road. Up those and on the right, a couple of hundred yards away, is the town, and a Tesco store, if needed. Beyond the bridge to the right is a huge mural - now somewhat faded - depicting the railway age without which Wolverton would scarcely exist. A sharp left-hand turn takes the canal briefly north-east. The line narrows into a throat at the start of a long embankment. Once solid, apart from a small opening for the stream, there is now a concrete aqueduct over Grafton Street, part of the Milton Keynes conurbation. This was installed in 1991.

At the next bridge the New Inn is across the water. The towpath here, and for much of the walk, is metalled, making progress easy. Wolverton is already behind, and open country takes over. For a few disconcerting minutes the line actually heads north before resuming its easterly thrust. There is a plantation of indigenous British woodland - birch, cherry, and alder being the more obvious - whilst at the water's edge evidence of the 1930s improvement scheme is seen. Unusually, there are two sections completed at

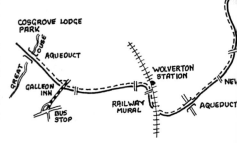

different times. One is inscribed "1931". A few inches away "1932" marks the next.

The Black Horse Inn is reached by bridge 76, serving a good range of food and drink. Beyond, a bridge crosses the water. This was once the Newport Pagnell railway line, known as "Newport Nobby", closed in 1967. The thirteenth-century tower of Great Linford church can be seen in the trees to the right, along with the grounds of the estate. This is worth a short detour from bridge 77. There is a very formal eighteenth-century manor house, and Dutch gabled almshouses. The whole area is a parkland of very mature trees and grass with gentle undulations, and displays a charm and elegance redolent of an earlier, more graceful age. Pass under the next bridge to reach Linford Wharf.

Linford Wharf to Newport Pagnell - 1¹/₂ miles

The private house here was once the Old Wharf Inn. To the left is where the Newport Pagnell branch left the main line. The edge of the canal bank clearly indicates its location. A factory now stands directly over the course.

But there are still things to see. Turn left, alongside the factory and directly away from the water. Cross what was the line before turning right down the lane. The cottage and depressions in the garden to the right indicate the one-time presence of locks. This is confirmed after a few minutes by a road name: Boulters Lock.

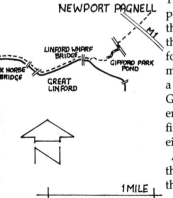

Through an iron gate, along a line of poplars, the shallow, waterless bowl of the canal is plain to see. Walk straight through the children's playground and follow the tarmac path, which has moved to the right of the trees, and after a few yards, water. Now known as Gifford Park Pond, it marks the effective end of the branch. Ahead, the remaining five locks and most of the canal are either built over or on private ground.

Although the canal is now infilled, there is still a little transport interest. By the bus shelter, a pathway under the road continues. This is the old railway again, and runs right into Newport Pagnell. There are a few artifacts still in situ lineside: mileposts and a signal mast. At the end of the path, in what was the old station, there are new houses directly ahead. Turn right to the road and then left. At the next road walk straight across along a wide alleyway which leads to Newport Pagnell Baptist church. Keep left of this, and the outward bus stop is a few yards along.

WALK 16 - OXFORD TO THRUPP - OXFORD CANAL

Due to its essentially rural character, meandering aimlessly for many a mile, there are not too many walks available on the Oxford Canal that fit the usual criterion: public transport to deliver you to the far end. There is a long walk to the south of Banbury - see Walk 17 - and another in the companion volume *Canal Walks: Midlands*. This one looks at the southernmost section of the canal.

The Oxford Canal was one of our earlier navigations and, for many years, a very important one. It connects with the Coventry Canal, just outside that city, and originally ran for 91 miles to the Thames at Oxford. James Brindley was the original engineer: that meant a contour canal. He died before the project was completed, and his assistant Samuel Simcox superintended much of the remaining work. Its value was soon obvious. The Midland coalfields were linked, via the Thames, to London and traffic flowed freely.

But not for long. The Grand Junction Canal opened a much more direct route to the capital from Braunston, whilst the Warwick and Birmingham Canal provided the second city with a direct route. But the Oxford fought back.

Between the end of the Warwick and Birmingham at Napton and Braunston was a $5^1/2$ mile linking canal: the Oxford. By charging extortionate rates to allow boats to use their short section they were able to remain a profitable company, despite the lack of trade. Coal still flowed along the northern section, but the meandering nature was causing time problems. By 1834 engineering techniques had advanced so far that the line was shortened. After completion of the works, the distance between the Coventry Canal and Braunston dropped from 38 miles to 23 miles.

Isis lock in Oxford lowers the canal into the Thames

The canal never suffered the dereliction that others endured in the 1950s and 1960s. Its essentially rural nature soon found favour with leisure boaters and today it is one of the most popular cruising lines in the country.

The towpath was badly neglected but recent initiatives from British Waterways have seen radical improvements, particularly on the summit level, and the whole line is now walkable.

BEFORE YOU START

WALK DISTANCE:	7½ miles
MAP:	OS Landranger Sheet 164
START:	The Boat Inn, Thrupp, east of the A423 Banbury to Oxford road
PUBLIC TRANSPORT:	Oxford is the nearest railway
STARTING GRID REF:	SP 481158
CAR PARKING:	Roadside on the lane or, with permission, at the Boat Inn
TRANSPORT:	Stagecoach Midland Red service X59 operates into Oxford. Details from 01295 253451
REFRESHMENT:	Oxford has everything. Several pubs littered

along the walk. Fast food supplies in
Kidlington, just off the route

NEAREST TIC: St. Aldates, Oxford OX1 1DY - 01865 726871

THE WALK

Walk back up the lane to the main road past some rather fine
housing, and at the junction, known as Thrupp Turn, is the bus stop.
On arrival at the bus station in Oxford, walk south to New Road,
turn right, cross Worcester Street into Hythe Bridge Street, and the
southern terminus of the canal is on the right.

On the left, across the road, is one of the newer colleges:
Nuffield, built in 1937. Before then it was the original canal terminus
with a basin, wharves and warehouses. But however strong the call
of the water, do not leave this city without a stroll round some of the
architectural treasures. There are 34 colleges for a start, plus churches,
the castle and a collection of museums and galleries to satisfy any
taste.

Oxford to Dukes Cut - 3 miles

The towpath here is on an isthmus, with river to the left and canal
to the right. At once, that delectable feeling of isolation takes over.
Here you are in a big city, with nothing but trees and boats. The
towpath is quite well used, and paved. After a few yards of casual
moorings, there starts a succession of house boats. Quite permanent
fixtures these, some with electricity supplied, and several with their
own letter boxes.

After a few hundred yards the towpath crosses over the neck of
Isis lock. This drops the canal down into the
Thames, and from here, the world is a boater's
oyster. Beyond the lock is Oxford station
and the remains of the old bridge

that crossed the river, causing so many boating hold-ups in years gone by. It slid across the river almost at water level, and moving it demanded railway staff with spanners to unbolt the track before others laboriously wound it open. The modern station buildings will be familiar to a host of people who have never visited the city. It, the canal a little further north, and much of the city centre have reached a whole new audience through the exploits of the cult detective series *Morse*, which brought to life Colin Dexter's thrilling books in the early 1990s.

Lots of other boats frequent this area. Some seem permanently moored, whilst others crowd around two boatyards on the far bank: Orchard Cruisers and College Cruisers. Beyond, elegant Edwardian town houses have long gardens reaching down to the water's edge. Many are well tended with elegantly manicured lawns; only the occasional one is neglected. And everywhere are willow trees, leaning right over into the water, seemingly aiming to get a better view of the boats.This can be a very busy water. At weekends newly hired boats set off, whilst throughout the week there are boats arriving from further north.

On the far bank there lies something of a culture shock. One does not associate this part of Oxford with the metal-bashing industries, but there they are, followed shortly by the expanse of the Unipart works. Here is the electric lift bridge, number 239A, which always seems to hold up someone rushing from factory site to factory site when a boat is passing. There are a few more drawbridges in the next mile or so, as the canal heads steadily away from housing.

The vast playing fields of St. Edwards School line the far bank. There are pitches for rugby, soccer, hockey and tennis; vast acres of green. Also here, on the towpath side, is a collection of houseboats. The towpath is churned up rather badly here, seemingly from the activities of the houseboat-dwellers. The railway has closed in on the left, and runs alongside for about a mile before, curiosity satisfied, it goes away and about its own business.

The very shallow Wolvercote lock leads into a busy section. The main A34 Oxford by-pass crosses overhead followed by Dukes Cut. That also gives access to the Thames. The lock down into the river is just beyond the railway bridge to the left.

Dukes Cut to Thrupp - 4 miles

Along this section, British Waterways often use a dredger. Many hours of corporate thinking time must have gone into naming this boat: *Dredger 1* !

In open countryside now, the walk is never peaceful for too long as both railway and main road north both draw near frequently, and then leave again. Kidlington Green lock marks the end of a relatively straight canal. From here, a sharp left takes the water under the railway, past Roundham lock, and into a series of twists and turns before a sharp left brings the walk back to Thrupp.

Just before, there is another splendid pub worth trying, the Jolly Boatman offering Morrell's beers. There are always lots of boats moored here, and with a lift bridge on a sharp corner, often some fun and games as less experienced boat crews try to deal with a heavy lift bridge and the inevitable wind blowing straight up the cut. Look out for one boat that moors here. It rejoices in the delightfully punnish name of *Thrupp'ny Peace*.

That terminates the walk, but you cannot possibly leave the area without journeying a couple of miles to the west. Here is Blenheim Palace, birthplace of Sir Winston Churchill, and the churchyard at Bladon close by which holds his mortal remains. The palace itself is quite magnificent, built in 1722, and is open every day throughout the summer.

WALK 17 - LOWER HEYFORD TO KINGS SUTTON - OXFORD CANAL

One of the problems of trying to produce one-way walks on the Oxford Canal is the lack of return transport. This beautiful line passes through some pretty remote countryside during its 77 mile route, with public transport at a premium. But the railway system helps out along this section which is one of the more attractive lengths of canal on this line.

A look at the history of the Oxford Canal will be found in Walk 16.

BEFORE YOU START

WALK DISTANCE:	9 miles
MAP:	OS Landranger Series Nos 151 & 164
START:	Kings Sutton rail station
PUBLIC TRANSPORT:	Chiltern Line trains to the station.
	Nearest intercity rail and coach stations are at Banbury
STARTING GRID REF:	SP 494360
CAR PARKING:	At the station
TRANSPORT:	Chiltern Line trains from Banbury to Oxford. Details from local railway enquiry offices
REFRESHMENT:	Very sparse. The Great Western Arms at Aynho Wharf is the only canalside refreshment. Boatyards there and at Lower Heyford offer drinks and confectionery, but little else
NEAREST TIC:	8 Horsefair, Banbury, Oxfordshire OX16 0AA - 01295 259855

THE WALK

Lower Heyford station is right alongside the canal. Join the towpath and turn left - north.

Lower Heyford to Somerton Deep Lock - 4 miles

The whole of this walk is in the valley of the River Cherwell, and both water courses are never too far apart. Indeed, for one section, canal and river flow together: more of that later.

The boatyard opposite is a popular mooring place for private boats, with a thriving hire fleet operating during the summer. Soon, the canal curves round to the right, carefully following the contour. This was a Brindley-built canal, and his obsession with holding contours at the expense of earthworks is well known. In the days when canals were first built, speed and time were not as crucial as they have since become.

There are houses on the right bank, but they are not numerous, each having rather splendid gardens. One even manages a great tree house overhanging the canal, which must give great delight to the children who use it.

Around the corner, the canal edge is well piled, allowing boat crews to dismount and work the fiendishly heavy-looking drawbridge. But appearances deceive. The whole thing is carefully balanced and works quite easily.

Another lock, set in the most delightful countryside, follows. Beyond, the countryside opens up a little and the railway crosses overhead. Until quite recently, this was an area offering the most appalling assault on one's eardrums due to a large air force base to the east. Upper Heyford was home to some extremely noisy jets, and the runway used to start just over the rise in the ground. Now the "peace dividend" has seen it close, and the screaming jet engines silenced for ever. The canal, at least, is a better place for their departure.

Bucolic Oxfordshire at its very best is revealed above Heyford Common lock. The gently rolling hills, bosky riverbank and occasional pretty dwelling all combine to produce this English idyll.

The railway comes alongside again as the walk approaches Somerton. Past the road bridge, the canal curves away to the right to dodge the hill whilst the railway carves straight through it. The lock ahead is Somerton Deep; with a rise of 12ft, it is well named.

Somerton Deep Lock to Aynho Wharf - 2 miles

The isolated former lock-keeper's cottage here must be a dream place for anyone with a dislike of neighbours, or a desire to crank up their stereo to full throttle! The difficulty of access from a road would discourage all but the most determined.

Continuing northwards, there is little to divert attention away from the canal: rustic and rural is a description that says it all. A lift bridge around the next right-hand bend leads towards a more wooded section, again with the railway close. The village of Clifton lies to the left, straddling the Cherwell, and can be accessed from the next fixed bridge by Wharf Farm. There is a pub in the village, but not much else.

A line of moored boats on the right-hand bank announces the approach of Aynho Wharf. Here, there

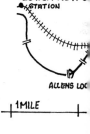

LOWER HEYFC
STATION

ALLENS LOC

1MILE

is another hire boat company, again with a shop, and the only canalside pub along the walk.

Aynho Wharf to Nell Bridge - 1½ miles

Boats continue to crowd in this section, but the actual village is almost a mile to the right. Shortly, the railway starts to do a few strange things.

This was once a very busy junction as the old Great Western line from Paddington to Birmingham and beyond met the Cherwell Valley line. The flyover that brought the down London trains over the Cherwell Valley line is still in use today, but the huge signal box that once controlled traffic is now no more.

This activity temporarily diverts attention from the canal. It shouldn't. There is an intriguingly shaped lock ahead. This is Aynho Weir lock, falling a mere 12 inches. Beyond, the River Cherwell crosses from one side to the other on the same level. The reason for this unusual shape is that the canal below needs a supply of water which a standard sized lock of 1ft drop would not give. So, to supply the extra, this large area was built.

A wooden footbridge crosses the river and leads to the last waterside section of the walk. This is straight - for once - and some ½ mile long. Approaching Nell Bridge and the lock there is no towpath, and the walk reaches a gate into the road. Here it is necessary to leave the canal as, although Kings Sutton and the canal are quite close further along, there is no way across either the Cherwell or railway.

Nell Bridge to Kings Sutton - 1½ miles

Turn right, follow the road and take the first left turn. Cross the M40

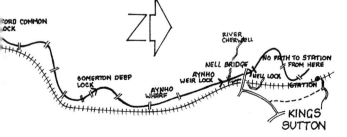

bridge and continue to the first Public Footpath sign on the left. There is a clearly defined and well used path, aiming just to the left of the church spire and towards the village of Kings Sutton. Dropping down a slight slope, close to the first housing, a meeting of the ways is reached. Take the left-hand path from here which leads through a coppice, down the bank and to a road. Turn left, and the station is just around the corner.

Chapter 4:
Greater London and Hertfordshire

WALK 18 - BROXBOURNE TO HERTFORD - LEE AND STORT NAVIGATION

A definite plus to this particular walk is that the railway follows the line of the river, giving a choice of three possible return points before Hertford. This can be useful should the weather deteriorate. For this reason, the usual practice of riding out and walking back is reversed. Much of the walk is in the Lea Valley Park, a mecca for north Londoners and locals who fish, walk, and generally enjoy pleasant relief from the frenetic pace of life hereabouts.

The River Lee has a long history of navigation. The Romans used it, and there are navigation Acts dating back to the thirteenth century. As early as 1571, a pound lock with mitred gates was built at Waltham Abbey. The following century saw the waters being used by London for drinking, a condition that obtains to this day. Trading boats on these upper reaches were never too common, although nearer London there was considerable lighter and barge traffic. Now, it is exclusively leisure boating.

BEFORE YOU START

WALK DISTANCE:	8 miles
MAP:	OS Landranger Sheet 166
START:	Broxbourne rail station, off the A1170, east of the A10 London to Hertford road
PUBLIC TRANSPORT:	As above
STARTING GRID REF:	SS 123456
CAR PARKING:	At the station
TRANSPORT:	Excellent service on Liverpool St to Hertford line. Details 0171 928 5100
REFRESHMENT:	Both ends, and pubs en route
NEAREST TIC:	The Castle, Hertford, Hertfordshire SG14 1HR - 01992 584322

THE WALK

Leave Broxbourne railway station and turn left. Walk east on the B194 towards Lower Nazeing, and after ¹/₂ mile, cross the river and turn left, upstream.

Broxbourne to Feilde's Lock - 2 miles

The tone of this walk is set in the first few yards. The river is wide and feels somehow impersonal. But you are never short of company, weekends at least. It's a popular area for both anglers and dog exercisers. And, Glory be, anglers along here are not given to using roach poles, which means a clear passage for walkers - splendid! Tree lined, there are gravel pits either still in use or flooded for recreational purposes, and the towpath is in good condition virtually all the way.

The first lock is only a few hundred yards along. Carthagena has a lock-keeper's cottage that is quite grand. Built in the 1930s by the Lee Conservancy, it's a very good looking, spacious residence.

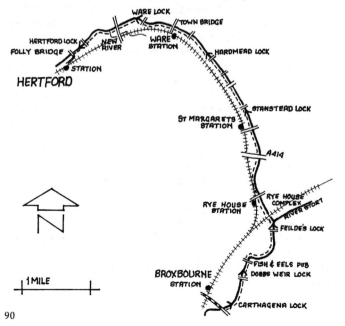

There are a number of cottages to the right between the towpath and a gravel pit. Some are clearly weekends only; some more substantial. One of these, made from wood, is burnt out and must have created quite a blaze when it went.

A road now crosses the canal with traffic controlled by lights. The delightfully named Fish and Eels pub is on the opposite side, well worth a break for refreshment. The river takes a sharp turn right here and a bridge takes the path across to the left-hand bank over an extremely modern and intricate weir.

Just before the next lock, Feilde's, the towpath leaves the river for a few yards to cross an arm that gave access to a basin at the site of the now demolished large power station.

Feilde's Lock to St. Margarets - 2 miles

Above the lock is the confluence of the rivers Lee and Stort. The latter bears right towards Bishops Stortford, whilst the Lee keeps to the left.

Around this point, it is possible to wonder about the size of the mosquito population. What started as a low drone rapidly becomes a huge volume of noise. Beyond the railway bridge, all is revealed. Across the water is the Rye House complex where you can see Kart racing, buzzing like the demons of hell, whilst nextdoor is the raw explosive blast of speedway bikes as four anonymous figures in helmets and gaily coloured leathers hurtle around a shale track. By the bridge here is the first opportunity to curtail the walk. Leave the towpath and turn left to Rye House station, just a few yards away.

Suddenly the river is a little smaller and more intimate. It's as though it's finished playing at being a river, and wants to become a canal. The departure of the Stort ensures that it succeeds. Beyond Rye House, the trees fall back, and the view across the valley can be seen for the first time.

Housing and some industry is confined to the left side here, with fields stretching away to the right. The river bears off right, and the channel actually becomes a canal. New development is visible on the edge of Stansted Abbots as the walk approaches a bridge with the A414 overhead. Here is St. Margarets station, and the next break point.

Hertford, on the River Lee

St. Margarets to Ware - 2 miles

Also along this section, the overhead power lines, which have persisted for some way now, swing off and leave the river in peace. Stanstead lock is followed by Hardmead lock as the railway closes in tight. Still relatively rural, this pleasant state is soon to end as the path approaches Ware. One last opt-out point is here by Town Bridge. Again, left, and a few yards away is the station.

Ware to Hertford - 2 miles

For the last section of this walk, the canal/river has turned sharply left and is now heading generally south-west. The river is joined again above Ware lock before the line plunges under the fiendishly busy A10. Just beyond, keep an eye open for a small run-off on the towpath side. Appearing rather insignificant, it is the start of a gargantuan piece of engineering; at least, for its time. In the early 1600s London's drinking water, taken from the Thames, was so foul that a fresh supply was vital. The New river was cut from here to the city. Straight lines and wooden aqueducts were features of this work that is still in use today, albeit only as far as Stoke Newington.

Ahead is Hertford lock and Folly Bridge. Leave the river here, turn left and follow the road round to the railway station.

WALK 19 - SAWBRIDGEWORTH TO BISHOPS STORTFORD - LEE AND STORT NAVIGATION

Still in the Home Counties, this short walk explores the River Stort section of the Lee and Stort Navigations. For a location so close to the great metropolis, it can be delightfully secluded; provided you keep clear of a sunny summer weekend. A brief look at the history of these navigations can be found in Walk 18.

BEFORE YOU START

WALK DISTANCE:	5 miles
MAP:	OS Landranger Series No 167
START:	Bishops Stortford rail station
PUBLIC TRANSPORT:	Excellent rail service to the town
STARTING GRID REF:	TL 492209
CAR PARKING:	At and around the station
TRANSPORT:	Regular service on the Cambridge to London Liverpool Street line
REFRESHMENT:	Only in Bishops Stortford
NEAREST TIC:	The Castle, Hertford, Hertfordshire SG14 1HR - 01992 584322

Sawbridgeworth to Spellbrook Lock - 2 miles

Leave the station platform, join the road and turn right across the railway. There is a bridge crossing a small offshoot of the main navigation before a larger bridge over the main river. The towpath is a large wide affair that leaves to the right.

The path soon narrows, but remains well walked as trees crowd in and the grass gets deeper. On the other bank is campshedding after the style of a true canal with a selection of buildings beyond. Already the walk has become remote with buildings diminishing quickly. Those that are left are quite Kentish in appearance with a clapboard exterior. There are specific comparisons to be made with the buildings of Walks 5 and 6. Sawbridgeworth lock soon appears and passes without undue attention unless there happens to be a boat working through at the time.

Allotments take over the far bank now, as the towpath remains pretty with quantities of trees. A line of moored boats adorns the river, and a low iron bridge takes a different footpath over the water and away before the railway grumbles across overhead. This is the line from Bishops Stortford to Sawbridgeworth and is an exceptionally busy suburban line, the more so since Stanstead Express service was introduced.

It is a dedicated service with coaches in a distinctive livery. It runs from Liverpool Street direct to the airport in about 40 minutes, with around two trains an hour.

Isolated and rural now describes this section. The river meanders gently, first closing up to the railway, then, having decided that the noise is too much, galloping away again into seclusion. But, like a curious child, it is tempted back for another look.

The towpath crosses the river proper to enter a canalised section. This leads to a rather bleak looking Tednambury lock. Unfortunately, concrete sides and open vistas do nothing to complement the image of beauty that has gone before; with a name like that, it should have more to offer.

More boats can be seen moored on the right. They are hiding in the old section of the river, off what is now the main channel. Cross a bridge where canal and river rejoin and continue up the still clearly defined path. Another $1/2$ mile or so and the walk meets the first road since the start.

Sellbrook Lock to Bishops Stortford - 3 miles

Another lock, Spellbrook, and the road is soon left behind as peace reasserts itself quickly. Plenty of trees, particularly willow, add to

SAWBRIDGEWORTH

STATION

SPELLBROOK LOCK

WALBURY CAMP

TEDNAMBURY LOCK

TWYFOR LOCK

RUSHYMEAD NATURE RESERVE

1 MILE

the scene. Another decrepit old bridge takes a path to the left, cracked brick abutments with a railed cast iron deck.

The river continues to wind in a most attractive way with little evidence of the world outside until another bridge appears in the distance, around - inevitably - a long and sweeping curve to the right. On reaching the end of this section, a stile leads off the towpath into a road.

Turn left, cross the road and pick up the path, clearly marked the Stort Walk Way. This is a confusing area of conflicting water movements, but the towpath stays on the right-hand bank, along a long wooded footbridge over a weir and alongside Twyford lock. Beyond, trees form an almost complete cover overhead. With those on the far bank, this is particularly attractive in autumn when the various hues meld to make a quite distinctive picture.

The path leads into an area designated Rushymead Nature Reserve. This is a series of what appear to be irrigation ditches in the trees. They actually preserve part of the River Stort Flood Plain forming a living record of social and natural history. The site covers over 10 acres, and has been summer grazed for thousands of years. There was also a sewage pumping station earlier this century, but that is now history. The area has been colonised by a wide variety of flora and fauna. A pictorially descriptive board a few yards into the woods adds flesh to this bony narrative.

At South Mill lock the start of Bishops Stortford is noted; but only just. It does not intrude at all for the moment, the walk staying pleasant and peaceful, aided in no small measure by the continuing abundance of trees.

At the lock a bridge below the tail takes the towpath to the left-hand bank. This section above the chamber is home to more boats, again, mainly moored. It is a strange fact that,apart from weekends,

there is very little actual movement on the water. Approaching a much more elaborate wooden bridge, the main river plunges off to the left. Cross under the railway and there is a significant change to the walk. A busy main road is first heard, then seen, its intrusion emphasised by what has gone before.

The path eventually converges with this road. Cross and turn right. Walk up the road a short distance to another Stort Way signpost which indicates the continuance to the left. The towpath is now back to the right-hand shore and continues along a metalled way, the backs of small factories to the right, elegant housing to the left.

At the next road bridge leave the water, turning right, and join a road by the Rose and Crown pub. Pass the bus station, with another pub, the Falcon, across the road, and turn right to the station approach.

WALK 20 - ST. PANCRAS TO PADDINGTON - REGENTS CANAL

This is an opportunity to visit our nation's capital and explore free from tourists. There is lots to see on this short walk, so allow plenty of time. Parking is a nightmare; even at weekends it is never easy. The solution adopted by this writer, as with any visit to London, is to park on the outskirts near an underground station and come in on the tube.

The $8^{1}/_{2}$ mile long Regents Canal was planned by a local businessman Thomas Homer. He saw the potential of linking the Grand Junction Canal, which had already arrived at Paddington, with London's dock area. The work was carried out with guidance from the famed architect John Nash. He planned the canal to encircle another project on which he was engaged: Regents Park, and appointed an engineer, James Morgan, to carry out the work.

As a friend of the Prince Regent, permission was obtained to name the canal after him. An Act was obtained in 1812, opening by August 1820. The line ran from Browning's Pool - named after the poet and now known as Little Venice - to the River Thames at Limehouse. The excavations resulting from the work, particularly Maida Hill tunnel, were used in the construction of Lords cricket ground which is a few yards to the north.

Trade was instantly attracted to the line, and continued to flourish as tonnages carried mounted. By the 1870s $1^{1}/_{2}$ million tons of freight moved along the canal. The arrival of railways did not have a marked effect on trade for some time; by the early days of the twentieth century, cargo of over a million tons was still moving. But the rot was setting in.

Diglis Basin, Worcester (Walk 21)
Saul Junction, Gloucester and Sharpness Canal (Walk 23)

Tiverton Basin, Grand Western Canal (Walk 25)
Bude Canal (Walk 26) *(Photo: W. Unsworth)*

A novel Chinese restaurant built on a barge at Cumberland Basin, Regents Canal

The company had worked closely with the Grand Junction over the years, and the two amalgamated in 1929 to form the Grand Union. Despite their best efforts, trade continued to fall away so that today the only movement is of pleasure boats. A further look at the Grand Union Canal can be found in Walk 13.

BEFORE YOU START

WALK DISTANCE:	4 miles
MAP:	OS Landranger Series No 176
START:	Paddington underground station
PUBLIC TRANSPORT:	The lot, and in profusion
STARTING GRID REF:	TQ 268817
CAR PARKING:	See above
REFRESHMENT:	Everywhere
NEAREST TIC:	44 Duncan Street, Islington, London N1 8BL - 0171 278 8787

THE WALK

Leave the underground at Kings Cross and St. Pancras and take the exit towards the latter. This then splits into either the station or St. Pancras Road; again, take the latter. At the top of the steps bear left into St. Pancras Road. The severe red brick of this edifice is alongside to the left, whilst the lighter - and cleaner - brickwork of Kings Cross station is across the road. Pause a moment and look up at the fascinating structure which is St. Pancras Hotel. This outrageously ornate building was constructed at the end of the last century and has been derelict for some years now. Recently some work has been done to preserve the glorious interior, and perhaps one day it may well open; a monument to the grandiose Victorian era.

Walk along St. Pancras Road, crossing to the right-hand side. As the main road bears left under the railway bridges, bear right into Goods Way, with several gasholders visible. At the end turn left into York Way, and a few yards along on the left, a flight of steps leads to the towpath.

York Way to Cumberland Basin - 2 miles

Turn right. Ahead is St. Pancras lock, but before reaching it there is a bridge over which the towpath passes. Underneath was an arm to the huge Great Northern Railway warehouse and interchange of freight used to take place here. There is also a conundrum. The iron parapet is deeply scored by the passage of a million towlines over the years. But at the far end a gently rounded iron coping is fixed. Here the ropes have slid over without making any impression. From appearances it would be reasonable to assume that this once covered the whole bridge: when was it removed, by whom

CAMDEN LOCK
DINGWALL'S WHARF
AVIARY
CUMBERLAND BASIN
MACCLESFIELD ROAD BRIDGE
LONDON ZOO
REGENTS PARK
LORDS CRICKET GROUND
MAIDA HILL TUNNEL
LITTLE VENICE
A40
N. WHARF RD.
PADDINGTON STATION
N

and why? In this area is a horse ramp, the first of three on the walk.

This is a break in the towpath edge with a slope down into the water. For whatever reason the towing horses would sometimes lose their footing and fall into the canal. Unable to climb out, they were led along to the nearest ramp where footing was available for them. There is one close by the railway out of Euston station. There, the shriek of a steam engine whistle would sometimes frighten the animal which bolted and invariably ended up taking an involuntary swim.

The lock was once one of a pair. This was needed because of the sheer volume of trade on the canal. The remaining chamber is cascaded and unusable. Above the lock, the St. Pancras Cruising Club have their base. This vibrant outfit, with lots of enthusiastic owners, organise group cruises in the summer when lots of their members get together to visit the less used stretches of canal.

The large spread of railway tracks that pass overhead, one of several such crossings on this walk, come from St. Pancras station. Once the Midland Railway's London terminus, their express services reached northwards to Leicester, Derby, Sheffield and Leeds and included famous named trains. The *Thames Clyde Express* and the *Thames Forth Express* ran to Glasgow and Edinburgh respectively every day. This diversity of service is now history, and Sheffield is the farthest north the intercity 125s now reach. There is also an intense electrified commuter service to Bedford.

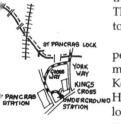

After several more road overbridges and a peaceful walk away from the frenetic pace of the metropolis, the next locks are reached. The first, Kentish Town, is followed closely by Hawley and Hampstead Road. This is the popular Camden locks area, and any peace and seclusion so far is now dramatically lost. In this area, which was once a timber wharf, there has been an explosion of interest which has brought small businesses in its wake. There is a first class pizza restaurant, several craft shops and a huge weekend market nearby.

Above the top lock a small diversion is necessary to cross the old arm that served

99

Dingwall's Wharf. Bear to the right until it is possible to cross the remains of this arm and then turn left back to the towpath. Another towpath bridge once crossed another railway interchange, this time belonging to the London and North Western Railway company.

The exit lines from Euston cross overhead, carrying trains to the north-west and Scotland. Soon there follows a sharp right turn. Cumberland Basin is on the left with a collection of unusual boats, none more so that the barge with a multi-storey Chinese restaurant. The Feng Shang Floating Chinese Restaurant is permanently moored here. The cuisine is reputed to be first class, and offers the chance of an unusual break on the walk. The actual basin was once the start of a southward reaching arm, stretching almost $1/2$ mile to a hay market just a few yards to the west of Euston station. It has long been disused, and was infilled with wreckage from the blitz.

Cumberland Basin to Paddington Station - 2 miles

Now starts the Regents Park section. This is one of the most delightfully unusual sections anywhere on the English canal network. The Zoological Gardens reach down almost to the water's edge on the far bank, whilst on the towpath side the modernistic Snowdon aviary can be seen. There are a huge number of exotic birds in this cage, but a little careful study will reveal that the local starling population have found ways in and help themselves liberally to whatever food is on offer. This section of path is kept neat and tidy, and with regular boat movements, if only the local trip boats, it has a wonderful feel to it.

Not far along here is Macclesfield Road Bridge, the fifth along the straight. This had a nickname amongst the old working boatmen: Blow-Up Bridge. In 1874 a barge laden with gunpowder exploded directly under the bridge, demolishing it completely. The three boatmen were killed and there was substantial peripheral damage.

At the end of the section are moored boats. These are clearly residential, with flowers growing alongside the towpath. There are also several ridges in the path where electric cables serving the boats are buried.

Another railway is reached, this time the line from Marylebone. Once the mighty Great Central Railway brought their trains into London here. Now, it is but a commuter line to Aylesbury. However, it still has an occasional moment of glory. For several summers recently there has been a steam operated service to Stratford-upon-Avon. Designed specifically for the visitor to England, they appeared to be well patronised. At the time of writing they have ceased to operate, but the word is that they may well be restored soon.

Beyond the next bridge the portal of Maida Hill tunnel looms. There is no towpath through, so the walk leaves the waterside up a flight of metal steps. Turn left at the top, cross over the portal and turn right. This brings the walk into Aberdeen Place. To the right is a rather ornate brick building, Crockers Folly, which is a pub. Walk to the end, cross the main road and directly opposite is a white cafe. Take the road to the right of this, Blomfield Road, and return to waterside.

Or almost. There are more boats moored here, and the actual towpath is closed. To the rescue is a footpath right alongside which allows appreciation of the work done in planting gardens both on boat roofs and alongside. Just before the next bridge is a break in the wall and a path down to the towpath proper. Pass under the bridge as the canal opens out to a junction at Little Venice.

At the next bridge the path crosses to the other side on an elegant iron bridge. Take this and turn left. Walk alongside the brick wall with iron railings on top. As they finish, take the flight of steps to the road. Carry on to the first bridge and turn left. Cross, turn left again and a few yards along is an entrance into a park on the left. Take this, bear left towards where the bridge abutment meets the water and regain the towpath.

Walk down the left-hand side of what is now the Paddington Arm of the Grand Union Canal, under the Westway, to where the path ends and moves away from the water's edge. Continue along the road to a junction. Cross and directly ahead is North Wharf Road. Walk down here, around a left-hand bend and beyond a coach and car park is a footbridge marked St. Mary's Hospital. This crosses the basin, affording a splendid aerial view of the water and boats.

Across the water, turn left towards the main building. On reaching it turn right along the front and down the steps to South Wharf Road. Turn right and, at the end, left into London Street. At the main road the entrance to Paddington underground is on the corner.

Chapter 5:
Worcester and Gloucestershire

WALK 21 - WORCESTER TO TIBBERTON - RIVER SEVERN & WORCESTER AND BIRMINGHAM CANAL

An easy mix of river and canal scenery and lovely Worcestershire countryside. The transport between the start and finish is not brilliant, but the variety of experiences on offer - fascinating and bold canal infrastructure, views and Worcester itself - make it well worth the effort.

The Worcester and Birmingham Canal was planned to provide an easier and quicker link between Birmingham and the River Severn with its connection to the docks and export markets in Bristol. After opening in 1815 it became a busy waterway and Worcester developed an enviable range of warehouses as trade that had previously gone up to Stourport and the Staffordshire and Worcestershire Canal came off the river into the city.

In 1874 the canal was bought by the Sharpness New Docks Company as trade declined. One of the last regular cargoes on the canal was between Cadbury factories at Bournville and Blackpole, on the north-eastern outskirts of Worcester. By the time that trade went, leisure boating was starting to make its presence felt, and the navigation never suffered the decay that other, less fortunate ones did. Although only 30 miles long it needed the construction of no less than 58 locks to get to the plateau on which Birmingham is built.

The Severn has been one of England's major river navigations almost since time began. Ever a difficult river to work, especially at the lower reaches, steady improvements and the cutting of the Gloucester to Sharpness Canal ensured that trade flowed freely and regularly; even today there are flurries of activity as far as Tewkesbury, although Worcester and Stourport are now effectively for leisure use only.

BEFORE YOU START

WALK DISTANCE:	7 miles
MAP:	OS Landranger Sheet 150
START:	Plough Road, Tibberton, a small village north-east of Worcester, east of junction 6 on the M5
PUBLIC TRANSPORT:	Worcester is nearest
STARTING GRID REF:	SO 906580
CAR PARKING:	Ample street parking available
TRANSPORT:	Go Whittle - 01562 822966 - and Midland Red West - 01905 763888 - services 352 and 353 to Worcester bus station. Infrequent
REFRESHMENT:	Good pub at the start, all services in Worcester; little between
NEAREST TIC:	The Guildhall, High Street, Worcester WR1 2EY - 01905 726311

THE WALK

The bus stop is about 50 yards away from the canal bridge beyond the Bridge pub, which sells an excellent glass of Banks's: a fine start or finish to your walk. Or, if you prefer, one at each end! In

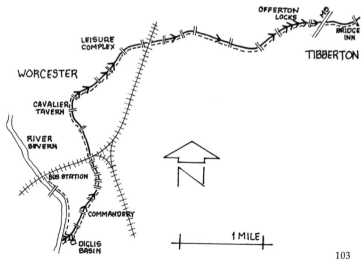

Worcester, leave the bus station and walk the few yards down towards the river. Turn left.

Worcester to Lowesmoor Basin - 2 miles

A stroll along the river front of Worcester is one of the more pleasurable experiences on our inland waterways. Ecclesiastical buildings overshadow everything. The magnificent cathedral, started in 1084, contains the tomb of King John, and the fifteenth-century St. Andrews spire riverside is 250ft high. There is always activity on the river. This can vary from a huge flock of swans to the large passenger boats, and plenty of canal craft leaven the mix. It's also very popular with oarsmen and women. From single scullers to rowing club eights, they are all "messing about on the river", and enjoying the experience. The path here is paved, and is a very popular walkway.

Reaching the point where the canal empties into the river, cross the water and turn left, walking up by the 2 Diglis locks. A fingerpost here advises that it is 32 miles and 58 locks to Birmingham. The expanse of Diglis Basin opens before you. Here, tiny little plastic boats, chunky steel narrowboats, veteran clinker-hulled sailing boats, and pristine white "gin palaces" all rub shoulders. And not one of them seems out of place: a thoroughly cosmopolitan area.

At the lock keeper's house, turn right, across the swinging footbridge, and follow the path round over the next bridge as though you are making to leave the basin. Almost at the exit gate is a toilet block (British Waterways key needed for access) on the left. Turn left down a little alleyway along the side of it, and regain the towpath.

The unkempt looking factory on the left-hand bank is actually the rear of the world renowned Royal Worcester porcelain works. This exquisite ware is on sale at the factory shop, and the Dyson Perrins museum in the city has a magnificent collection dating back to 1751. Mooring rings still in situ provide a hint of the canal's carrying past there from days gone by when boats used to collect and deliver.

Ahead lie the first lock and the Commandery. Originally a hospital, started at the same time as the cathedral, the present building was erected in the mid 1400s. It was used by Charles Stuart at the time of the Battle of Worcester in 1651, and is open to visitors. Well worth including in your walk.

The canal almost sneaks through Worcester now, past Blockhouse lock and with bridges coming in quick succession, the first of which takes the towpath to the left-hand bank. The narrow entrance to Lowesmoor Basin is crossed.

Lowesmoor Basin to Astwood Railway Bridge - 2 miles

Now a hire fleet base, this was once where much of the city's coal was unloaded after its journey from the Midlands. Here also is the oft photographed, high arched railway bridge carrying the old Great Western Railway line out of the city and off towards Hereford. For an essentially urban section of canal, there is still a remarkable amount of greenery around, with trees of all sizes and shapes. Also, keep an eye over your left shoulder; there are stunning views of the Malvern hills from time to time.

After an industrial start, lengths of attractive new housing have been built on both sides. Now, older rows of tenement houses reach the water's edge. After lock 5 the buildings start to recede. By 8 they have pretty well cleared. At bridge 13, the towpath returns to the right bank, and a flight of four locks follows. Then a large leisure complex occupies the left side with enormous cricket and soccer pitches. Around the perimeter is a paved track on which joggers abound.

Considering the amount of boating traffic the canal carries, it is remarkably weedy hereabouts. Which is really just a taster for the green which is now taking over the walk, and is the hallmark of this canal. Industry makes its last, brief attack on the eye as the walk reaches another railway bridge.

Astwood Railway Bridge to Tibberton - 3 miles

This railway is not as busy as it once was. Main line cross-country services from the north to the west used to travel this way as a matter of course. Now, they tend to use a line to the east, bypassing both Worcester and Droitwich. Beyond Blackpole lock, another road will accompany the walk for a short distance, but it is well shrouded by trees and not too intrusive. In the distance to the left, the tree lined Hindlip Park rises, looking very pretty. It is also possible to look back to the hills here, and realise how high you have climbed after just seven locks.

Six more locks lie ahead now, the attractive Offerton flight, scarred forever by the M5 motorway screaming overhead just beyond the top lock. But its assault on your aural senses disappear almost instantly as the canal enters a pleasant bosky cutting. The towpath deteriorates somewhat along this length, but recent bank improvement works will soon restore the path to normal. Another few hundred yards brings bridge 25 into view. Leave the towpath, turn right and back to the start.

WALK 22 - COOMBE HILL TO TEWKESBURY - COOMBE HILL CANAL & RIVER SEVERN

For this walk, the usual outward transport and return walk is abandoned. There are two reasons for this. Parking in Tewkesbury is difficult, and the view of that town as approached is magnificent. Walking away from it deletes that pleasure.

The River Severn has been navigable since man first climbed into a boat. Originally open from Bristol to the upper reaches, over the centuries silt has made much of the river unnavigable. Now the length from Avonmouth to Sharpness is used by coasters; from Gloucester to Stourport-on-Severn, commercial trade has all but disappeared. The leisure industry has the river almost to itself.

Indeed, even the lower reaches, treacherous with tide races and shifting sandbanks, are frequently used by narrowboats travelling to or from the Kennet and Avon Canal. Because this is a high-risk journey, pilotage is available and only the foolhardy venture out to sea - which, effectively is what it is - without an expert and radio telecommunications equipment.

Most sorts of cargo have used the Severn over the centuries. A special type of boat, the Severn Trow, evolved to carry freight. Sail rigged, they were bow-hauled by teams of men when the weather demanded. Coal from the Forest of Dean collieries was one cargo, and the desire of the worthy burgers of Cheltenham to buy it was the reason behind the construction of the Coombe Hill Canal. Opened in 1796, this $2^{1}/_{2}$ mile waterway, lock free save for one at the river entrance, was successful in its early days. It must have been a sight to behold as boats and bargees, wharfingers, carters and horses all milled around the somewhat cramped area.

As with most other canals, the coming of railways bit into trade; so much so that in this case the canal closed in 1876. For years it stood abandoned and unloved as nature started to reclaim her own. There were several proposals to infill, and as many to restore, but each came to naught. The most recent attempt was in the 1970s when a gentleman bought the whole canal privately. His idea for sympathetic restoration was balked by local conservationists who objected loudly to every move.

The project ended in abysmal failure, and the canal was bought in 1985 by the Gloucester Trust for Nature Conservation; the whole area is now called a Canal Nature Reserve. Fine. But compare this overgrown stagnant length of water with other canals where restoration has allowed boats and anglers use of the water. Sure, the Lesser Spotted Dungleworzul (or whatever) is saved for the occasional person who can find it, but boats and even anglers bring a life and vibrancy to other similar areas that this one totally lacks.

BEFORE YOU START

WALK DISTANCE:	7½ miles
MAP:	OS Landranger Series Nos 150 and 162
START:	Coombe Hill Canal Basin. This lies 300 yards west of the A38 Gloucester to Tewkesbury road at Coombe Hill. The turn is down a narrow lane alongside the Swan Inn at a set of traffic lights
PUBLIC TRANSPORT:	Gloucester is on the intercity rail network; Tewkesbury is served by National Coaches
STARTING GRID REF:	SO 887273
CAR PARKING:	Alongside the canal basin
TRANSPORT:	Stagecoach Cheltenham District service 41 (not Sundays) operates from Tewkesbury Abbey to the Swan Inn
REFRESHMENT:	Pubs en route, full selection at Tewkesbury
NEAREST TIC:	64 Barton Street, Tewkesbury, Gloucestershire GL20 5PX - 01684 295027

Coombe Hill Basin to River Severn - 2½ miles

Walk along the head of the basin and turn left, along the bank across from the car park. Heavy weeding makes the water invisible at times, whilst thick hedgerows obscure the view. But it is very peaceful; pretty without being stunning. It is also a bridleway, and horses have churned up the ground when wet, leaving it rutted and offering the chance of a damaged ankle to the unwary.

There is a narrow footbridge after about a mile which returns strollers to their cars. From this point, the going underfoot improves. At the next bridge a coffer dam has been formed, and the canal effectively ends. Alongside this are the remains of what was once a genuine canal bridge; alas, only the abutments are original.

The footpath ends a few yards short of the River Severn, at a road. Turn left along it, and 200 yards along is a bridge over a drain. On the right is a stile. Take this and head for the river. Turn right.

River Severn to Haw Bridge - 1 mile

For the whole of this length to Lower Lode, the path wanders somewhat, not always staying right alongside the water. There are innumerable stiles and gates,

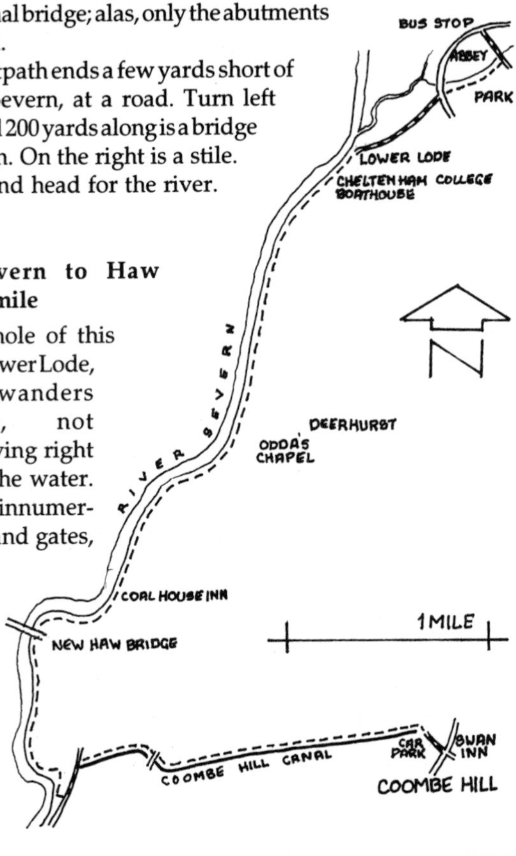

BUS STOP

ABBEY
PARK

LOWER LODE
CHELTENHAM COLLEGE
BOATHOUSE

RIVER SEVERN

DEERHURST
ODDA'S CHAPEL

COAL HOUSE INN

NEW HAW BRIDGE

1 MILE

COOMBE HILL CANAL

CAR PARK

SWAN INN

COOMBE HILL

the first one being after about 150 yards. Here, it is some 75 yards back from the river, and alongside the gate are the ruins of the canal's river lock.

Continue along the path, and the bridge at New Haw comes into view. This is quite a new structure, only built in 1961. There was nothing wrong with the previous one; nothing, that is, until a barge demolished it one storm-racked night in December 1958 when the river was in spate. On reaching it there is an option to turn left and cross the water for access to a couple of pubs.

Haw Bridge to Lower Lode - 3 miles

The walk continues along the right-hand bank, and soon another pub is reached, the Coal House Inn. It's a free house offering food as well.

One impression that soon takes hold on this walk is that the intimacy one associates with canals is lost amongst the sprawling river valley. Not that this detracts from the walk - far from it. It's just different. For one thing, there are no pretty towns or villages to pass through. They're there, but never too close to the Severn, with its well known propensity to flood.

The village of Deerhurst is a case in point. This can be reached by a short diversion along a footpath and contains the Church of St. Mary. Parts of this building date right back to 804, and it has one of the best preserved Saxon fonts in the country. The tower has double triangle-headed windows above the nave, and is well worth a visit. As is Odda's Chapel. This was built just before William conquered the country in 1066, and was used as a farmhouse for many years later. The stone recording its construction date of 1056 can be seen at the Ashmolean Museum in Oxford.

This is generally a lonely walk, with few people around, until Lower Lode is reached.

Lower Lode to Tewkesbury - 1 mile

Here people flock to both sides of the river, although ne'er the twain shall meet. A large boathouse on the right holds craft belonging to the prestigious Cheltenham College, as the path opens onto a concrete launching pad. Beyond, a narrow road starts away from the water's edge towards Tewkesbury.

River Severn at Lower Lode

Half a mile along, a new walk logo is attached to a post on the right. This is a rose with crossed swords: the Battle Trail. This refers to the bloody Battle of Tewkesbury fought on 4 May 1471. One of the most significant battles in the Wars of the Roses, this one saw the Yorkist army under King Edward IV rout a Lancastrian force gathered by the wife of Henry VI, Queen Margaret of Anjou, with the intention of installing her son Prince Edward of Lancaster as king. The exact location of the fight is not certain, but all contemporary accounts refer to Bloody Meadow. This starts a few yards along the footpath.

On reaching the road at the end, walk straight across into the park. This then becomes at least a walk alongside water; by the little River Swillgate. By now, the views of Tewkesbury Abbey have become overpowering. At the far end of the park, turn left into the road. Follow this to the main road at the top. On the left, in a small crescent, is the bus shelter.

With a little time in hand, why not visit the abbey? There has been a religious building on this site for 1200 years, the present one being over 900 years old. It was originally the church of the Benedictine Abbey of Tewkesbury, and was the last such to be

Tewkesbury Abbey

dissolved by Henry VIII. Around the corner are the Abbey Cottages. They were built in 1450 and are the only remaining ones of this type in the country.

WALK 23 - FRAMPTON-ON-SEVERN CIRCULAR - RIVER SEVERN, STROUDWATER & GLOUCESTER AND SHARPNESS CANALS

Unusually for a canal walk, this one involves a surfeit of directions. The "reach the canal, turn left and walk for 7 miles" most certainly do not apply here. There is also the opportunity to extend the distance by some 4¹/₂ miles by eliminating an overland section and staying with the river as it describes a huge loop. In addition, a mid-walk choice can shorten the shorter walk by another ¹/₂ mile.

The Gloucester and Sharpness Canal is some 16 miles long, lock-free, apart from one at each end, and can accommodate vessels up to 29ft beam and 190ft long. With trade on the River Severn increasing rapidly in the eighteenth century following burgeoning industrial activity which combined with the opening of the Staffordshire and Worcestershire Canal at Stourport, improved navigation was deemed vital to the efficient movement of trade south of Gloucester. Here the river was subject to shoals and frequent shifting of sandbanks, making sailing a boat something of a lottery.

An Act of Parliament was granted in 1793 allowing the construction of a canal from Gloucester to Berkeley Pill, 2 miles south of Sharpness, which effectively did not exist at that time. Gloucester dock and 5 miles of canal were cut before the money ran out. Work ceased, and nothing further happened until the government asked Thomas Telford to examine the area in 1817. He recommended that the line be built as far as Sharpness. Funding came from the state, and the whole line, then the broadest and deepest canal in the world, opened in 1827.

Trade flourished, and sea-going ships were unloaded in Gloucester Docks. Sharpness was improved towards the end of the nineteenth century, and ships up to 1,000 tons could then be accommodated. The canal was still carrying a considerable volume of trade, but as the size of boats increased, so the use of the Gloucester facilities died. Oil was a regular cargo for many years, and grain still moves intermittently today. Otherwise the main use is leisure.

The Stroudwater Canal was opened in 1779 to link the town of Stroud with the Severn; and beyond, the world. It had a long and useful life which expanded considerably when the Thames and Severn Canal - see Walk 24 - was opened in 1789. Its story is inextricably intertwined with that canal and is dealt with in that walk.

The Thames and Severn effectively closed in 1934, the Stroudwater lasting a further 20 years. Today, that late closure means that most of the 8 mile/12 lock line existed when the Restoration Age dawned.

Now reunited under the banner of the Cotswold Canals Trust, there are high hopes that the Stroudwater will eventually be restored in full. The story of navigation on the River Severn is told in Walk 22.

BEFORE YOU START

WALK DISTANCE:	6¹/₂, 7 or 11¹/₂ miles
MAP:	OS Landranger Series No 162
START:	Saul Junction. This lies 2 miles north-west of the A38 Gloucester to Bristol road. Turn off this at Whitminster and follow the sign for Saul. On crossing the canal at the swing bridge, turn right
PUBLIC TRANSPORT:	Virtually non-existent
STARTING GRID REF:	SO 756094
CAR PARKING:	Along the service road
TRANSPORT:	None needed
REFRESHMENT:	One pub at Upper Framilode. Another at Framilode
NEAREST TIC:	St. Michael's Tower, The Cross, Gloucester GL1 1PD - 01452 504273

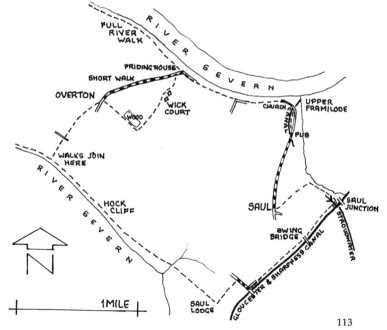

Saul Junction to River Severn - 1¹/₄ miles

The "crossroads" here was created in 1826 with the arrival of the Gloucester and Sharpness Canal. The footbridge over the Sharpness is actually over an old lock chamber, an indication of the amount of work needed before navigation on the Stroudwater could again be possible. For connoisseurs of these matters, the balance beams still in place are very similar in construction to those on the Leeds and Liverpool Canal. Turn left, and after only a few yards the remains of the line disappear under a field. Follow the waymarkers alongside the stream until it reaches a bridge. Turn left, cross a stile and into the field which is a farm track.

Keep to the right-hand edge, and when it reaches a stile to the right, take it and aim for the right-hand edge of the wall surrounding St. James's Church, Saul. This leads to a narrow lane with a road beyond. Turn right and continue until the ground starts to rise at a bridge. The Stroudwater is underneath and back in water. Cross the bridge and take the entrance to the left. This leads along the water's edge, past the Ship Inn, a Free House.

At the end of this section, the path returns to the road. Turn left, down to the river.

River Severn to Overton - 2¹/₄ miles

The attractive small church of St. Michael's, Upper Framilode, is almost alongside the river. Bear left with the road, which shortly disintegrates into a track and then, passing over a stile, to a footpath alongside but several yards away from the water. The arrangements along here are the result of an extended flood prevention scheme by the National Rivers Authority which was not completed until June 1995.

Another stile returns the track to something resembling a road, but this soon leaves to the left: follow the narrower road to the right, back alongside the river. Along here on the left is a huge farm decorated with a wonderful collection of old enamel advertising hoardings enjoining everyone to "Smoke Wills Wild Woodbines" or wash in "Rinso". These are augmented by street names, French "No Parking" and Spanish "No Fishing" signs: truly wonderful. And there is a huge pole in the garden with large wooden beer kegs hung from cross-trees, acting as nesting space for birds.

Delightfully decorated Priding alongside the River Severn

Shortly beyond Priding Farm is Priding House on the right. Here the road again turns away from the river. This is decision time. The full riverside walk continues straight ahead over a stile, adding $4^{1}/_{2}$ miles to the base distance. This will follow the sweep of the river all the way, meeting up with the base walk at *.

Bear left, and 150 yards later is the site of another decision. The shortest walk continues along the road, up the hill for around 500 yards and turn right at a Public Footpath sign. At this point the base walk will rejoin at **.

Turn left into the first gateway which leads into a field and gives access to the medieval moated manor house Wick Court. Through two fields, and the complex of buildings is on the left. Entrance to this site involves a left turn; the gate which would take the walk directly ahead is a slight dog-leg left.

The buildings are worth an examination. Currently under restoration with funds from English Heritage, the place will become a residential centre run by the charity Farms for City Children. The perry pear orchard is being restored, the ridge-and-furrow field systems retained, and fine work carried out breeding the distinctive Gloucester cattle, only a few decades ago virtually extinct. There is also a pack of mongrel dogs, noisy but seemingly friendly, Gloucester

115

Old Spot pigs, and poultry of every conceivable kind: everything running free.

Another point of interest is to be seen on the corner of the lane. The old oak tree must be all of 40ft around the base of the trunk.

In the field, walk towards the far left corner, and alongside a gate, but well hidden by undergrowth, is a stile. Keep the boundary of the next field close to the left and continue across this field towards the woodland. In the far left-hand corner is another stile; another straight ahead. This is into woodland, along the edge of a small coppice. At the far end cross the stile and turn right, heading up the gentle rise. In the far right-hand corner of this field is a stile; cross and continue straight ahead.

This leads over the crest of the hill, with an old Ordnance Survey triangulation point to the left. There is also a superb view. Half right, the Severn continues its way with Garden Cliff clear to see, the delicate spire of Westbury-on-Severn church a little further beyond. Over to the left is more river; the area the walk will soon reach. A clear path continues downhill over a series of stiles to a road.

Overton to Fretherne Canal Bridge - 2½ miles

Here a dog-leg left will reveal another stile and Public Footpath sign. It is also where the road walk meets up again.

** Take this, but ignore the clear path ahead and take the lesser one to the left around the perimeter of the field which leads to a farm track. Directly across is another stile, the route of the walk. At the end of that field turn left, and right by the next field boundary. This leads to a small footbridge over a ditch, across a field and up the flood bank to the Severn. Turn left, and meet up with the long river walk.

* The walk now follows - more or less - the course of the river for well over a mile. But not before a hilly section alongside Hock Cliff where the view is redolent of a coastal footpath. It continues to be signed the Severn Way, even as the river takes off to the right whilst the path continues straight ahead. A left turn close to the elegant Saul Lodge brings the track back to a road and the canal bridge. Immediately on the left, just before crossing, take the towpath.

Fretherne Canal Bridge to Saul Junction - 1 mile

Continue along the towpath. Halfway along is another swing bridge, but quite different to the one at Fretherne. There the bridge keeper lowers barriers to stop the traffic by hand, and then cranks a huge wheel to swing the bridge. At Sandfield a few pressed buttons and the whole sequence is carried out automatically.

WALK 24 - SAPPERTON TO STROUD - THAMES AND SEVERN CANAL

This is one of the classic canal walks, albeit beside a currently derelict canal with very little water, and major blockages for the restoration team to solve. But, taking in the glorious scenery along Golden Valley, it really is a walk to be savoured.

The Thames and Severn Canal was originally conceived to link the Midlands with the River Thames and London. Building on the success of the Stroudwater - see Walk 23 - that company had a route surveyed in 1781. It was greeted with joy by many of the ironfounders from the industrial Midlands who saw the potential for their trade.

An Act was obtained and work started. The biggest engineering barrier was the need to tunnel at Sapperton. The completion of this delayed the through opening by nearly two years, but by April 1789 work was complete. Sadly for the company, success was short-lived. The Oxford Canal opened just eight months later, offering a far shorter journey from the Midlands to London.

Trade never approached the figures the company had projected, and, combined with a chronic shortage of water, navigation was never easy. Profits were poor, and eventually, after many devious machinations, the Great Western Railway obtained control.

The Great Western Railway version of care equated to absolute neglect - not that the Thames and Severn was singled out for special treatment. Great Western Railway policy was uniformly enforced unless there was any trade originating that could be funnelled to rail. They announced closure plans in 1893. This created consternation locally and the three affected councils, together with local businesses and other local canal companies, formed a consortium to take over. Despite further expenditure, mainly to try and staunch the water leakage, trade faded.

For restoration? A hard slog, but boats will pass this way again one day.
Thames and Severn Canal

The last loaded boat over the summit was recorded in 1911. Trade was virtually gone, and the line from Puck Mill Wharf westwards to the Thames was abandoned in 1927. After last-ditch efforts to save it, the rest was abandoned 6 years later.

In 1972 the Stroudwater Canal Society was formed, becoming a Trust three years later with the addition of the Thames and Severn. Now the Cotswold Canal Trust is charged with managing both lines, and is working steadily towards through restoration. That this will be achieved is certain: but the projected date - well into the next century - means that the prospect of watching boats again is very far off.

BEFORE YOU START

WALK DISTANCE:	9 miles
MAP:	OS Landranger Series No 162
START:	Stroud bus station
PUBLIC TRANSPORT:	Regional Railway service to Stroud station, National Coaches to the town centre
STARTING GRID REF:	SO 851053
CAR PARKING:	Car parks around the town
TRANSPORT:	Service 54 - Stroud to Cirencester is operated by Stroud Valley Stagecoach. Details from the TIC
REFRESHMENT:	Several pubs en route, everything in Stroud
NEAREST TIC:	George Street, Stroud, Gloucestershire GL5 1AE - 01453 765768

Sapperton Village to Sapperton Tunnel mouth - ½ mile

Alight in Sapperton village by the school and take the road to the left close by. This drops downhill, past St. Kenelm's Church which is worth a few minutes' exploration. Unusually, many of the gravestones have metal labels, making identification by the curious more easy. Some of the tower is original Norman construction, dating back to around 1100, but the rest has been rebuilt over the centuries. That said, much of it is as craftsmen of the fourteenth century left it: remarkable. Even the youngest of the three bells in the tower dates back to 1698.

Inside, the impression is of an unusual amount of light. This is helped by the absence of stained glass in the windows save for the east one. An intriguing connection between St. Kenelm's and the canal is to be found in the church register. The ordered continuity of rural village life, the same names appearing for generations, is suddenly shattered by the arrival of navvies to dig the tunnel. After the work was over many stayed on, married local girls and settled down here. This sudden influx of different names has never been repeated.

Walk down the lane to a stile on the left. Cross this, work diagonally left down the steep hill to another stile, concealed by the boundary hedge. This leads to a path which crosses the north-western tunnel portal and turns left to gain the towpath.

Sapperton Tunnel Mouth to Chalford - 4 miles

Sapperton is the third longest canal tunnel in the country at 3,817 yards long. It was cut 14ft wide and 15ft high. A fall inside has blocked it and entry is dangerous and forbidden.

The towpath is wide and firm, although the canal bed is totally dry. Trees and hedges crowd the pathway, giving shade in summer, and making the most stunning display in autumn. Indeed, the whole of this walk has an extra dimension added when the leaves are changing colour. Shortly, the walk reaches the Daneway Inn whose car park is built on the site of a lock chamber. The path continues along the side to a road. Across the road, continue on the right-hand side of the waterway.

The canal has been looked after by the Gloucestershire Wildlife Trust since 1964; which will doubtless create problems when the canal is eventually restored as boaters

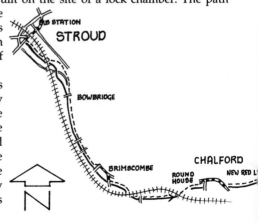

and conservationist interests clash.

The Sickeridge Wood flight of locks follows. Here, west of Brimscombe Basin, the chambers are 71ft long and 12ft 3ins wide, dropping around 8ft on average. Soon a bridge takes the towpath back to the left bank, there to continue its delightful way. Lock chambers punctuate the walk with great regularity. Beyond this point, the valley starts to widen a little and the trees recede: up to this point this has effectively been a woodland walk.

After a cluster of houses at Puck Mill, the towpath returns to the right-hand bank over an accommodation bridge. To the right is a reservoir. This was once a series of millponds until the canal people arrived and converted it to store water for their use. The stream sharing the valley with the canal is the River Frome, and its power was once harnessed both here and at several other points downstream.

Approaching Chalford, the chance of refreshment is offered by the New Red Lion on the right, whilst the towpath continues through trees again to arrive at the main road. For a short distance now, the canal is lost under roads and factories. Turn right and walk along the main road for some 200 yards, past the bus shelter, to a left turn. Cross this, and immediately on the left corner is a narrow unsignposted pathway, opposite the war memorial. This leads past one of the distinctive round Thames and Severn houses back to the canal: and water.

Chalford to Stroud - 4½ miles

The stream that has accompanied the walk for much of its way is, by now, becoming much larger. After about 200 yards there is another infilled section with garages built across the bed where a lock chamber once existed. Follow the notional line of the water to regain the towpath proper.

Just before the next lock the railway closes in on the left. Here, and at several other points along the walk, it is possible to see boundary markers. These are large metal posts with round flat iron plates on the top and inscribed

121

"Great Western Railway Cos". The railway crosses to the right-hand side as the walk passes through a low tunnel lined with corrugated iron and comes out at the next lock chamber.

Approaching Brimscombe, the canal actually starts to look like a waterway again. The water is crystal clear, moving, and holds a few trout. This happy state of affairs does not last long before the cut becomes slower moving. Another culvert under the railway, and beyond, the path follows the Frome for a short distance. This leads to a service road and into an industrial estate on what was once the canal interchange basin at Brimscombe. Here, trows from the Severn could penetrate, but the lock size beyond accommodated Thames sized barges, hence the transfer. There were wharves, sheds, company offices and agents' houses, and associated buildings, all built between 1806 and 1809. Up to 100 boats could be handled at once.

On reaching the road bridge that turns left over the river, bear right and walk towards the large stone building. On reaching the water turn right alongside it. This is part of the old basin. Walking towards the offices of Fenworth, a plaque on the wall notes the history of the site. Turn left at the end of the water and follow the road to the left around a brick warehouse and continue as far as the road. Ahead is the Ship Inn. Walk straight across, keeping just to the right of the pub into a lane.

This soon peters out into a track. Carry straight on, ignoring the wider track leaving to the left up a slope. This is again the line of the canal, as will soon be seen. Note the lock; plainly a different size to the ones that have gone before. This is Severn Trow size, 72ft by 16ft 6ins.

Reaching Bow Bridge, a circular weir on the right is unusual in this corner of the world, although similar ones can be seen on the Staffordshire and Worcestershire Canal, walks of which feature in this writer's *Canal Walks - Midlands*. The lock alongside also has the remains of paddle gear at the top end. Beyond this chamber it is necessary to leave the canal and cross a road before walking down the other side to continue. The Frome closes in very close and, beyond, the path leaves the canal up a slope to a road. Just before the road bear left, under the railway arch, to another path where a fork will be seen. Keep to the unmade path to the left which leads under

A round house, famous landmarks on the Thames and Severn Canal

the new road and back waterside.

After 8 miles of canal in varying degrees of decrepitude, on the final few yards of this walk there is some real sign of restoration work. Upper lock is complete and in working order, and the area around what was Stroud Wharf is tidy - although surrounded by new roads. This is almost the end of the Thames and Severn; a little further along it makes an end-on junction with the Stroudwater Canal, which once provided the link to the Severn.

Leave the canal here, turn right over the water, past the Bell Hotel, and straight up, under the railway and into the town. Where the main road turns right, a lane to the left gives access to a precinct with the bus station at the far side.

Chapter 6:
The South West

WALK 25 - TIVERTON TO SAMPFORD PEVERELL - GRAND WESTERN CANAL

All that remains of the Grand Western Canal are 11 lock-free miles from Tiverton (Devon) heading north-eastward to Lowdswells. The western end, strictly speaking the Tiverton Branch of the Grand Western, offers glorious Devonian scenery combined with a wealth of canal interest.

The Grand Western Canal was a constituent part of an impressive plan to link the Bristol and English Channel, eliminating the hazardous journey around Land's End. This canal would run from Topsham, near Exeter, where it would join the River Exe, to Taunton where it would link into the Bridgewater and Taunton Canal. Three branches, to Tiverton, Cullompton and Wellington were also proposed. Work was started on the summit level - which meant no locks needed building - in 1810, and by 1814 a short length was ready, along with the Tiverton Branch. Barges started to trade.

As was usual in canal construction - and has carried over to many civil engineering projects today - the cost vastly exceeded the estimate, and the company was left short of cash. A new engineer, James Green, was recruited to build - as cheaply as possible - the link to Taunton, whilst the westward proposals were abandoned. Green, never a fan of locks, introduced an inclined plane and seven vertical lifts to change levels. As Green's work will be referred to again in this chapter, a look at his ideas here is apposite.

The idea of an inclined plane instantly reduced the size of vessel that could be used. These tub boats, as they would become known, carried about 5 tons, and had wheels on the bottom. They were towed through the water in trains by horses and, on reaching the plane, were uncoupled and hauled up the slope by rope into the higher water level to continue their journey. They were slow, severely restricted the weight that could be carried, and the hauling machinery was never reliable. In sum, they "seemed like a good idea at the time".

This section opened in 1838, but by 1844 the Bristol and Exeter Railway had opened, offering a much faster transit time. The tub boat section closed in 1869, but the summit, together with the Tiverton Branch, continued to carry barges well into the twentieth century.

The canal was taken over by Devon council in 1971. Since then, they have maintained it and the whole original length is available for walking.

BEFORE YOU START

WALK DISTANCE:	7 miles
MAP:	OS Landranger sheet 181
START:	Tiverton Parkway rail station
PUBLIC TRANSPORT:	As above
	National Coaches also serve the town
STARTING GRID REF:	ST 046139
CAR PARKING:	Ample space in the station
TRANSPORT:	Tiverton and District service 373 Cullompton to Tiverton (not Sundays). Details on 01271 45444
REFRESHMENT:	All services in Tiverton. Pubs in Halberton and Sampford Peverell
NEAREST TIC:	Phoenix Lane, Tiverton, Devon EX16 3BG - 01884 255827

THE WALK

Catch a bus at the stand just outside the station door and alight at Tiverton bus station. Walk back to the traffic island and turn left on Great Western Way. Cross, and after a few yards a gateway on the right gives access to a path which runs alongside, but climbs above the road. At the next traffic island turn right up Canal Hill. A couple of hundred yards up the hill on the left is the Canal Basin.

Tiverton Basin to East Manley Aqueduct - 2¹/₂ miles

This is quite a centre for tourism. Two horse-drawn trip

126

boats, one a genuine old narrowboat butty *Hyades*, provide visitors with boat rides, and a couple of small day boats are available for hire. Immediate evidence of the canal's *raison d'être* is clear: limekilns. And, with the canal above them, it was easy to discharge directly into their tops. Limestone came from quarries near Holcombe Rogus, and for years was virtually the only traffic on the line.

Leave the basin, with fine views across to the town, and sharp bends give early notice that this is a contour canal. The towpath is usually well frequented here, not least by younger people. Blundells School is near Tidcombe Bridge. Founded in 1604, famous *alumni* include R.D. Blackmoor who set the opening of his novel *Lorna Doone* at the old school building, now a private National Trust property, and John 'Jack' Russell, the hunting parson and dog-owner.

One fine feature of this walk is an abundance of seats along the towpath. They are quite rudimentary, being a couple of vertical wooden supports carrying a railway sleeper. Most carry an inlaid plaque acknowledging the sponsor. Beyond East Manley, the usual limit for the trip boat, the canal crosses an aqueduct under which the railway to Tiverton used to pass.

East Manley Aqueduct to Samford Peverell - 3½ miles

The town used to be served by a diminutive tank engine, wheezing along with a couple of coaches to the main line at Tiverton Junction. The branch fell victim to Beeching in the 1960s, and the Junction station closed in the 1980s, replaced by Tiverton Parkway,

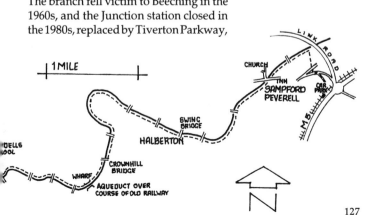

127

a mile to the north, but with extensive parking facilities and good access from the M5 and A361. An old wharf lies just beyond the cast iron aqueduct trough.

Crownhill Bridge takes the towpath to the south side, where it will remain for the remainder of the walk. Under the next road bridge, the canal turns sharp left near a milestone, and then describes a huge arc to the right before reaching Halberton. It was on the approach to this village that the Great Western Railway, who bought the canal in 1864, installed stanking in 1924, ostensibly to eliminate leaks, but in fact closing the canal.

After Devon County Council took over responsibility for the line in 1971, it was removed, and modern techniques used to waterproof the bed. The canal passes through a cutting, under a fixed steel bridge known as Swing Bridge(!). If thirst calls, leave the towpath and walk down the hill to the road, turn right and, after a few yards is a rather dowdy looking Welcome Inn. Its appearance is acknowledged on a board outside:

DON'T BE PUT OFF BY THE PEELING PAINT
COME INSIDE AND HAVE A PINT

Past the bridge is a quarry where the sandstone used in the canal's construction was cut. It was here that the eminent canal historian Charles Hadfield lived as a child, and this was the canal that first fired his imagination and curiosity. On through rolling countryside to Sampford Peverell and the start of an exquisite length of canal, full of water fowl, and past St. John the Baptist Church, its gaunt squat tower typical of the county's churches.

There is a winding hole here, and just beyond, a wrought iron gate leads down to the Globe Inn, a pleasant refreshment stop. After another 600 yards take the gate on the right, just before the new road overbridge.

Sampford Peverell to Tiverton Parkway Station - 1 mile

Walk down the lane, straight across the road at the end, and bear left at the next T-junction. This leads back to Tiverton Parkway rail station.

Counter balanced paddle gear on the Bridgewater and Taunton Canal

Beam Aqueduct, Rolle Canal (Walk 29)
Maritime museum, Exeter Canal basin (Walk 30)

WALK 26 - BUDE TO MARHAMCHURCH - BUDE CANAL

We are well into the west for this delightful walk; effectively the only Cornish canal remaining with any water in it. The original thinking behind the Bude Canal was a link between north and south coast, eliminating the Land's End passage. Whilst of little note today, when this canal was conceived almost 200 years ago sail was the only method of propulsion. Tide races and unpredictable winds around the end of Cornwall saw ships founder regularly, and hundreds of lives were being lost every year.

The concept was to create a canal from Bude that headed inland for some miles before picking up the Tamar valley. Then, at a spot near Launceston, it would join the river, eventually ending in Plymouth. The link was never completed, but the Bude still had quite a life in its own right.

Authorised by Act of Parliament in 1819, the $35^1/2$ mile canal was opened in 1825. Construction was over difficult terrain and involved some massive engineering works: particularly inclined planes. James Green was the engineer in charge. However, the whole canal was not built to tub boat standards.

The sea lock in Bude can take boats of up to 300 tons, and from there, for the next 2 miles, barges could work: until they reached the first inclined plane. There, freight was trans-shipped into tub boats. Agriculture provided most of the business, which meant that there was never much profit for the promoters. Sea sand and limestone were carried inland; produce returned. The arrival of railways quickly rendered the canal obsolete, and it was finally closed in 1901. Most of the line is now back in private ownership, but much evidence of its existence can still be found. Indeed, almost a century later, the barge section still holds water.

BEFORE YOU START

WALK DISTANCE:	4 miles
MAP:	OS Landranger Sheet 190.
START:	Marhamchurch, to the south-west of Bude
PUBLIC TRANSPORT:	Poorly served

STARTING GRID REF:	SS 223036
CAR PARKING:	Streets close to the church
TRANSPORT:	Service provided by W.J.O. Jennings Ltd leaves from the shelter by the front entrance to the church. Enquiries on 01288 352359
REFRESHMENT:	Pub in Marhamchurch, everything in Bude, nothing between
NEAREST TIC:	The Crescent, Bude, Cornwall EX23 8LE - 01288 354240

THE WALK

Catch the bus and alight in Bude by the Bencoolen pub. From there, walk straight ahead along The Crescent. As the road swings to the left to cross the canal, turn right along the wharf and out to the sea lock before turning back inland.

Bude to Hele - 2½ miles

To those more used to the usual type of canal, it is a culture shock to realise that here is a partially operational canal that locks down straight into the Atlantic Ocean, next stop New York! It's the only canal in the country to do so. The bottom gates are normally left open, and huge chains secure the top gates against the possibility of high tides forcing them open.

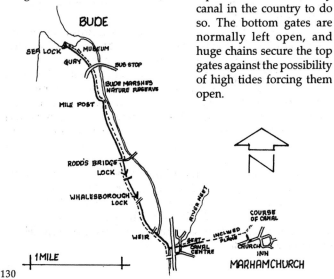

Along the quay it is possible to pick out the remains of a narrow gauge railway. This used to run down onto the beach where sand was collected and loaded into boats for delivery inland. Sand was a very useful item to farmers in lightening the clay-heavy soil and increasing the depth of tilth.

The Bude-Stratton Historical and Folk Exhibition on the quayside is well worth a visit. It has lots of artifacts and pictures of shipwrecks on the surrounding coast, testimony to the awesome power lurking just beyond those lock gates. Tied to the quay and looking thoroughly at home is a converted working narrowboat. It is now a Christian bookshop deliciously named Ark Angel.

Walk across the road and through the gate following the towpath. A sign here informs that this is the Bude Marshes Local Nature Reserve. The water is wide and weed free with the River Neet never far away, very close on the left.

A reed bed in the river basin is home to a diverse collection of birds. Cormorant, little grebe. seagulls, a range of hedgerow birds and a motley collection of hybrid ducks are all likely to be seen. A hide has been constructed beside the towpath to assist in observation over the marshes. The graffiti inside, without being offensive, indicates that nature study of a very different kind takes place in there after dark!

The only blot on this delightful horizon is the town's gasholder. Round a sharp left-hand bend the first canal milepost can be seen. Cast iron, squat and stubby, it carries the legend "1 Bude".

The towpath changes sides over a lowered bridge where one of the many notices that festoon this canal can be seen. This threatens terrible retribution on dogs and owners should they even think of fouling. As both appear illiterate, careful placement of dainty size 11 walking boots is needed.

Rodd's Bridge, the first lock, is reached. All four gates are missing, but a V-shaped concrete wall at the head maintains the water level in the higher pound. The paddles are still operative, the old hernia-inducing direct lift: no fancy gearing for those sturdy old Cornishmen. The capping is clean cut granite whilst the walls are unusually built from random stone. A strange effect compared to the more traditionally built stone chambers that can be seen on locks up-country.

Whalesborough lock follows quickly, and then the canal starts to take on a thoroughly unkempt appearance. Round the next bend the cut changes into a canalised river with a large weir opposite and the A39 ahead. Improvements to this road some years ago changed the complex nature of this area where rivers and canals shot off in different directions. Now, cross the road and the canal is the right hand of two bridges opposite. Examination of the brickwork reveals rope scoring, mute testimony to the horses and men that once laboured on this waterway.

Hele to Marhamchurch - 1¹/₂ miles

The character of the canal changes yet again here. The path is now a tree lined glade, with the water dark and weedy. There is never any shortage of seats for a break on this walk, and one of particular interest is located just by the start of this new section. Presented by the Inland Waterways Association, it recognises outstanding fundraising achievements, on their behalf, by Dr. A.J.C. Sandek of Truro.

Before long the water course is almost obstructed by an earth bank. A further 30 yards and the water finishes for good, and there arises an unusual problem for the regular canal walker: a hill to climb. This was the site of Marhamchurch Inclined Plane, over 800 yards long and lifting boats 120ft. The path continues up alongside, although much of the land has now been reincorporated into fields and private gardens. The small factory on the left here produced all the ironwork that was needed when the canal was constructed.

At the top of this incline the path bears right. Pause awhile here (if only for a breather), lean on the fence to the right and try to imagine horses, men, tub boats and winding gear: all the things that made this such a busy spot. The course of the canal goes off to the left through private fields, whilst the walker must follow the path to the end of the lane and turn left to the church, 100 yards away.

It is possible to explore the canal further. Turn left by the Bray Institute to the public footpath 100 yards on the right by Old Canal Close. This was the towpath, but it peters out into nothing a few hundred yards further and leads nowhere.

A couple of miles' drive away is the site of another inclined plane at Hobbacott, once the second largest in the country. This is at grid reference SS 244049 on the A3072 Stratton to Holsworthy road. Access is through a farm gate in a lay-by formed from the old road. The basin, buildings and slope are still visible.

WALK 27 - TAUNTON TO BRIDGEWATER - BRIDGEWATER AND TAUNTON CANAL

This is the longest walk in the book, but it does cover the full length of a canal, an unusual feat to achieve.

The Bridgewater and Taunton Canal was conceived as a ship canal, linking Bristol and Exeter, eliminating the hazardous passage around Land's End. The "grand plan" was never realised, and the Bridgewater and Taunton was constructed for barges with the unusual dimensions of 54ft x 13ft. The original length, from Taunton to the River Parrett at Huntworth, on the edge of Bridgewater, opened in 1827. The extension into Bridgewater itself did not come about until 1841. The Grand Western Canal built their link from Taunton to Tiverton, but using only tub boats - see Walk 25. By the time these canals were open, the railways were making their presence felt, and canal mania was a thing of the past.

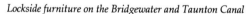

Lockside furniture on the Bridgewater and Taunton Canal

Trade was adequate, but never made a fortune for its shareholders. The Bristol and Exeter Railway bought the line in 1866, and the last tolls were collected in 1907. Bridges were fixed when the swinging mechanism was removed in 1940, and Bridgewater docks closed in 1971. The locks down into the River Parrett were sealed, and the whole line left to fester away. But the leisure explosion on our waterways up-country was mirrored here in the west. The Somerset Inland Waterways Society was formed in 1966 to support the line, local councils took an interest in the amenity value, and restoration is a reality: apart from the link to the Parrett. All the bridges are restored to navigable height and, with the final work being completed in 1995, boating is now possible on the whole length.

BEFORE YOU START

WALK DISTANCE:	14¹/₂ miles
MAP:	OS Landranger Sheets 182 & 193
START:	Bridgewater rail station. The town is to the west of the M5 junction 23 southbound, 24 northbound
PUBLIC TRANSPORT:	See above
STARTING GRID REF:	ST 308369
CAR PARKING:	At the station
TRANSPORT:	Regular train service to Taunton
REFRESHMENT:	All services at each end. Pubs en route
NEAREST TIC:	50 High Street, Bridgewater, Somerset TA6 3BL - 01278 427652. The Library, Corporation Street, Taunton, Somerset TA1 4AN - 01823 274785

THE WALK

Catch the train at Bridgewater station and alight at Taunton. Leave the station, turn left at the main road, and walk to the first set of traffic lights. Here, with the Crown & Sceptre pub on the corner, turn left into Priory Bridge Road. Cross the River Tone and immediately turn left down a flight of steps to the river bank.

Taunton to Creech St. Michael - 3 miles

Follow the river past the first bridge, and cross by the second, over the weir to the left-hand side, which brings the walk to the shallow (1ft 6ins) Firepool lock, the start of the canal. Turn right and keep to the right-hand side of the canal. The towpath is wide and good, paved, and a shade higher than the river on the right. Although there is no trade on the canal now, at the Obridge Bridge there is mute evidence of its existence. The abutment has iron capping, deeply rope scored. The first mile is through the industrial end of Taunton, with ready mixed concrete plants and some retail warehouses. The word "industrial" is relative in this corner of the system. Compared to the Birmingham Canal it is positively rural, the cut still lined with willows; and attractive it looks, too.

Once past the outer edge of Taunton the towpath degenerates into something of a bog, particularly during rain. After the first mile Priorswood Bridge is reached. This was the last fixed obstruction to through navigation. At Bathpool is the British Waterways work yard, and close by, the pretty Monkton Road swing bridge. The housing development on the right replaces a delightful complex of buildings that was St. Quentins. Once a farm, it transmogrified into an archetypal canalside business

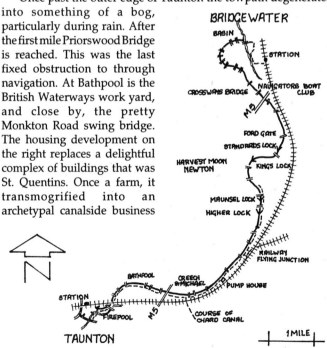

135

renting boats and cycles, with a tourist information room, a shop and a park for both static and touring caravans. Just as the canal became fully navigable again, the whole lot disappeared.

Just before the M5 motorway makes its noisy way overhead there is a pretty old thatched roof building with elegant topiary and an ancient greenhouse, small panes of glass on a deep and very rickety whitewashed brick base. Approaching Creech St. Michael, on the right, an embankment heads off to the south, just beyond the remains of a wartime pillbox.

This was once the Chard Canal, which fed traffic into the Bridgewater and Taunton, but had a very short life. It was an intriguing amalgam of tunnels, inclined planes and locks. James Green was the engineer, and, as was his way, it was a tub boat canal - see Walk 25 for details of this system. It opened in 1842 and was sold to the Bristol and Exeter Railway in 1867. They had just opened a branch to the town, and closed the competition in the following year. At the junction there used to be a bridge and stop lock, but all traces have long since disappeared.

Creech St. Michael to Maunsel Lock - 3 miles

The railway comes very close as the walk approaches Charlton. Between rail and water is a decrepit old building. It was built to house steam engines that used to pump water from the Tone, just beyond the railway, into the canal.

Fields to the left are planted as orchards. Depending on the time of year, they are either stark bare branches, a swathe of blossom or laden with ripe red fruit. All cider apples, they are bound for the local cider presses for which Taunton is famous.

Then an interesting railway structure comes into view. Lines from the west country to Paddington and Bristol diverge here, at Cogload Junction, and the westbound line from Bristol leaps over the London tracks to form a flying junction.

The first of a pair of locks hoves into view. Higher lock has a plaque on the top gate noting that the western branch of the Inland Waterways Association contributed to the cost of installing safety ladders in the chamber. Above Lower (or Maunsel) lock, boats are moored. The locks are well maintained. The top paddle gear is fascinating: ungeared but with large cast iron balls attached by chains as counterweights. On the bottom gates the gear looks like ground paddle gear but is attached to the gates in gate paddle style; a curious amalgam.

Maunsel Lock to Crossways Swing Bridge - 5½ miles

At Newton Swing Bridge a signpost points to the Harvest Moon pub in the village. It is ¼ mile away and offers home cooked food and real ale. Kings lock, which follows soon after, has concrete balance beams on its top gates, and Standards lock is about a mile further along.

One feature of this canal which insinuates itself on the unconscious is the staggering number of wartime pillboxes lining the towpath; at least thirteen. Most are of concrete and well overgrown. One, near Fordgate, is different. Set on a bridge-like narrows, it is actually alongside, and controlling the water. Directly across are huge pyramids of concrete which acted as tank traps. These were all established in 1940 as a defence against invasion, which seemed quite real at the time. They stretched along the whole of the south of England, and can also be seen on Walk 1.

The first canalside pub is discovered close to the M5 crossing on the outskirts of Bridgewater. Called the Boat & Anchor, it has a garden and the usual accoutrements. The motorway provides a roof for a myriad activities. Underneath can be found an extensive caravan store, stables, a vehicle restorer with a pre-war Ford Popular, late 1950s vintage Bedford vans and a double decker bus. Here the towpath changes sides on the pretty Crossways Swing Bridge.

Crossways Swing Bridge to Bridgewater Basin - 2 miles

On the right was the point where the canal originally joined the River Parrett. Known as Factory Arm, there used to be a basin, but of it there is now no trace. Urban Bridgewater now starts to impinge on the walk, and the towpath quality improves again dramatically. The canal enters the long stone walled Albert Street Cutting. The walls are sheer and so decrepit that they need huge timber cross-bracing to hold them in place.

The shallow Newtown lock drops the canal into the old dock basin area. There is plenty of mooring, but with very little moored: around 12 boats. Bowerings Animal Feed Works is a remnant of the past, whilst some attractive waterside flats are very new. Called Admiral's Wharf, it is named after the famous Cromwellian Robert Blake. There is a museum in town devoted to this old seadog, Bridgewater's most famed son.

Bridgewater Docks to Rail Station - 1 mile

Leave the basin area to the right, cross the bascule bridge and walk to traffic lights. Bear half left here, through a car park, past the Job Centre, and turn right at the end, alongside the river, to the first bridge. Turn left into Eastover, straight across at the traffic lights into St. John Street. After 300 yards the main road turns right. Walk straight ahead and the station is just around the corner.

WALK 28 - LUMBURN TO TAVISTOCK - TAVISTOCK CANAL

It does not take much contact with this canal to realise that it is every bit as attractive as the alleged frontrunners in the Beautiful Canal stakes. The Llangollen, Caldon and Mon. & Brec. lines are the ones usually favoured by the arbiters of public taste.

They should visit the Tavistock. For sylvan scenery on a contour canal, bosky hillsides, elegant stone infrastructure and wildlife in profusion, this canal is the equal of any. What it does not have is boats. Not quite. There is an enterprising company based in the town who offer canoe hire. This is a super way to see some of the canal, although passage along the more exciting bits is not allowed.

Transport of copper was the primary reason for the promotion of the Tavistock Canal, with deposits found at Mary Tavy, 4 miles to the north-east. Morwellham, on the River Tamar 4¹/₂ miles away, was an established port through which most of the metals won from this productive corner of the kingdom were shipped.

The progenitor of the work was 24-year-old John Taylor, a self-taught engineer who built a canal with a lock, aqueduct, an extremely long (2,540 yards) tunnel and the longest inclined plane in the country. He also used the canal's water to provide power for the machinery at mills and mines en route.

His scheme was to construct a canal 16ft wide and 3ft deep using

The picturesque course of the Tavistock Canal

tub boats, almost their first application in the south-west. An Act was obtained in 1803, but the work took 14 years. The major cause of the problem was Morwelldown tunnel, though not for the obvious reasons. No sooner had construction started than copper was discovered. This led to a mine being opened up alongside, and many other lodes were found. One of the smallest bore tunnels ever dug, it was hewn through solid rock.

With the canal complete, goods flowed in both directions. Coal and limestone came from South Wales up the canal, copper and slate returning. The copper was despatched as ore to South Wales for smelting, providing a handy return load for the schooners and ketches trading in the area.

Shortly after, the Millhill Branch opened, leaving the canal near the east portal of the tunnel and heading north for 2 miles to reach a slate quarry. This length also involved the construction of an incline plane. It was not a particularly successful investment and closed in the 1830s.

As the mines became exhausted, so trade died. Arsenic replaced copper for a short time as the main cargo, but the canal fell into disuse by the end of the 1880s.

It lay derelict until the 1930s. Then a saviour appeared, but without even a hint of altruism. The West Devon Electric Supply Company decided to install a hydro-electric generating station in the Tamar valley. This was opened in 1934, supplying Tavistock and the surrounding area with environmentally friendly energy.

To instal this equipment meant the construction of a 1 million gallon reservoir near to the western portal of the tunnel. The canal was dredged, various blockages removed, and a short new channel cut from the tunnel mouth to the reservoir. The company is now National Power and their generating station, in the Tamar valley close to Morwellham Quay, produces 640kW of electricity from two turbo-alternators.

BEFORE YOU START

WALK DISTANCE:	3 miles
MAP:	OS Landranger Sheet 201
START:	Tavistock, on the A390 Liskeard to Okehampton road in the west of Devon
PUBLIC TRANSPORT:	National Coaches. Nearest railway is Plymouth or Gunnislake
STARTING GRID REF:	SX 479743
CAR PARKING:	Several parks around the town
TRANSPORT:	Western National bus service number 185 runs from Tavistock to Bere Alston. Sleep's Coaches of Tavistock also operate a service. Details of both from Devon Bus on 01392 382800
REFRESHMENT:	Tavistock only
NEAREST TIC:	The Town Hall, Bedford Square, Tavistock, Devon PL19 0AE - 01822 612938

THE WALK

The bus station is on Plymouth Road. Ask the driver to put you off near the Caravan Club site where the road turns off to Newton. Or walk. The outward section is only $1^1/_2$ miles, but it is along the busy A390 road with only an occasional footpath. Leave in the Plymouth direction until you reach the huge statue of Tavistock's honoured son Sir Francis Drake.

Turn right by the statue, and left at the mini-roundabout at the top. This is the A390 Callington Road. A church stands to the left, the Catholic Church of Our Lady of the Assumption. Built from local granite in 1867 with a steeply pitched slated roof, the gaunt exterior belies a very attractive interior. There is a pavement for the next $1/2$ mile on the right, but after that, nothing.

The road drops into the valley of the River Lumburn, and shortly after the bridge is an entrance on the left, just on a sharp left-hand bend which is marked "Public Footpath".

The Millhill Branch - $1/2$ mile

This is the course of the Millhill Branch. At the other side of the road is a slope where an inclined plane took the canal to the quarries. Its exact location is now a matter of some doubt, as is the rest of the top section. As it is all on private land, the chance to put speculation to the test is not available.

Walking down the lane and through a gate, the bed of the canal

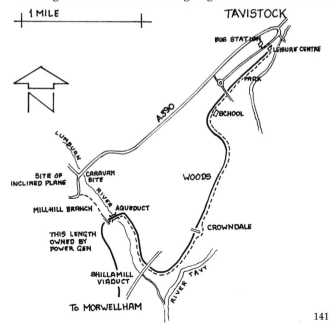

has been infilled, but it is soon possible to pick up the course on the right as a shallow depression. Then the main line is reached. A low bridge crosses the water. To the right, which is private and owned by PowerGen, the canal runs alongside the river valley before turning sharp right and heading into a steep sided deep cutting which leads to the tunnel. The old entrance to Wheal Crebor Mine is still clearly seen just to the right of the portal. Tens of thousands of tons of copper were produced during its lifetime.

Lumburn to Crowndale Farm - 1½ miles

At the junction turn left. The canal, quite narrow on this section, crosses the River Lumburn. One feature of this canal makes an impact immediately. Those used to the gentle, almost non-existent current on a canal are in for something of a culture shock as the water flows at a speed resembling a river.

The towpath along this section leaves something to be desired. It can be very muddy in inclement weather. Although the trees obscure the view somewhat, this is actually an aqueduct over the river; quite an impressive construction given its age. At the far end the line swings sharp right. In the left-hand corner is a device that looks quite like an old mangle. It is really a sluice to allow control of the water level. Round the corner the canal widens to something nearer normal.

There are several trees laid across the canal, blown down by the winds that can whistle alarmingly up this valley. One in particular, just before the railway, was a gnarled old elm. A victim of Dutch Elm Disease, it fell, blocking the towpath as well. Rather than attempt to clear the lot, a 3ft section of the trunk has been removed, leaving space for towpath walkers.

The elegant stone span of Shillamill Viaduct was constructed by the London and South Western Railway Company as part of their plan to reach Plymouth. It was opened in sections between 1865 and 1890, and involved a climb to 950ft just north of Tavistock. It was the highest point on the London and South Western Railway (later Southern Railway) network. From then, rivalry between that company and the Great Western Railway for fastest journey from London to Exeter and Plymouth was intense, and saw some fine express trains crossing this viaduct.

Inevitably, it fell victim to the Beeching axe when it was decided that the ex Great Western route to the south of Dartmoor was a better proposition. The last train passed along here on 5 May 1968: a sad fate for a scenically beautiful and handsomely engineered railway. A section of track in Tavistock has been bought by the council and made into a walk.

There is more remote countryside for the canal before it reaches a pretty but small stone bridge. Do not pass underneath but walk up to the parapet. There is an information board giving details of Sir Francis Drake. To the right, behind some rusty old railings and a patch of gorse, is the site that is rumoured to be his birthplace.

Crowndale Farm to Tavistock - 1½ miles

Crowndale Farm was established in the mid-fifteenth century, and survived a fire in 1549 before being pulled down in the 1850s. It was in 1588 that Drake was said to have been playing bowls on Plymouth Hoe when the Spanish Armada was sighted. "We have time to finish the game and beat the Spaniards" is the remark attributed to him. Looking to the left beyond the bridge is more evidence of the old railway line, up on an embankment with a high arched opening through it for farm use.

From here into Tavistock the canal is marketed by the local council as Drakes Walk. A gate alongside the current farm building marks the start of this length. It is through sylvan woodland, with ample views of the rolling Devon countryside. It leads to a section redolent of the Llangollen to Trevor Canal in Wales. Hewn out of a rocky hillside, the trough clings precariously to the contour, weaving wildly as it does so.

Approaching the town, the towpath quality improves, first into hard compacted stone and then to a metalled surface. Ahead is a busy road bridge, with no towpath underneath. Leave the path, walk up to the road, and directly across is a gate which leads into the last section of the walk.

This is extremely attractive. A well laid out and tended park occupies the space between canal and the River Tavy, some yards to the right. The canal bottom is clear of the usual detritus associated with urban water, and a large collection of mallards all patrol, demanding sandwiches with menaces.

At the far end is a large new building, the town's leisure centre. Pass to the left of this, but behind the canalside buildings. Walk through the car park to the right, and turn left into Canal Street. At the end is Plymouth Road and the bus station.

WALK 29 - TORRINGTON TO BIDEFORD - GREAT TORRINGTON CANAL

It is just a tiny bit improper to include this as a canal walk, the Great Torrington (or Rolle) Canal having being abandoned back in 1871 and infilled. But there is lots of water to walk alongside, the bed of the canal, and some fascinating remains to examine.

In 1823 Lord Rolle employed James Green to construct a 6 mile canal from Torrington to north of Weare Gifford, using the western side of the Taw valley. The whole project was funded by His Lordship, who met an eventual bill exceeding £40,000. Because of this the canal was - and still is locally - known as the Rolle Canal. The words Green, Tub Boats and Inclined Planes were synonymous - see Walk 25 - and so it proved here.

The tub boat canal would leave the River Torridge at a lock near Annery. From there it would proceed up the valley, climbing some 40ft en route to a terminus at Town Mill below Great Torrington. The two major engineering works needed were the inclined plane at Ridds and an aqueduct at Beam to take the line to the west side of the valley. The canal opened in February 1827, and there is evidence that the inclined plane was always troublesome to operate during its short lifetime.

A $2^1/_2$ mile southern extension was proposed to Cleave Marsh, but, as this would have involved further expensive earthworks and another inclined plane, the plan was never adopted in its entirety. A section by Healand Docks was built, almost a mile long, and this provided an additional source of water for both the canal and mills.

Limestone was shipped across the Severn estuary from west Wales, the coal to burn it coming from the South Wales collieries. Sailing boats tied up at Appledore or Bideford and the cargo was trans-shipped into waiting barges for transport to Sea Lock, there to discharge into tub boats for onward transmission. Previously, limekilns had been built only where the ships could reach with their cargo. Now they could be located along the canal, nearer to the point of consumption.

The railway, meanwhile, had arrived in Bideford, and there was a strong public movement in Torrington for it to be extended to that town. There then developed a situation arguably unique in the annals of canal history. The London and South Western Railway Company applied for and obtained an Act to construct a railway from Bideford to Torrington.

When faced with the true cost involved, they changed their minds and asked Parliament for powers to abandon the project. Rolle argued forcefully against this: a canal owner fighting for a railway to be built. In the end he won, and permission to abandon was refused.

With the railway forced to build, the reason for Rolle's unusual position became clear. He offered the London and South Western Railway the bed of his canal for their track. This would result in a far less costly construction, and the railway company agreed. Construction work commenced in May 1870, and the canal closed soon after. Much of the northern end disappeared under the railway, most regrettably the inclined plane at Ridd.

BEFORE YOU START

WALK DISTANCE:	7^{1}/2 miles
MAP:	OS Landranger Sheet 180
START:	Bideford rail station (closed but intact) in East the Water. This is up the hill by Bideford Bridge
PUBLIC TRANSPORT:	Trains to Barnstaple, National Express to Bideford
STARTING GRID REF:	SS 457263
CAR PARKING:	Outside the station
TRANSPORT:	Bus to Torrington Town Mills service 75 or 86 - details on 01271 382800. There is a frequent service to the Puffing Billy, 1^{1}/2 miles into the walk. This is service 70, pick up the walk at *
REFRESHMENT:	RHS Rosemoor, two pubs en route and all services in Bideford
NEAREST TIC:	Victoria Park, The Quay, Bideford EX39 2QQ - 01237 477676

THE WALK

Walk over the river bridge and turn right to the bus stops. Alight at Town Mills. At this point the canal crossed the road, and the path in front of the mill was the bed of the canal. By walking a little way along the B3220 it is possible to see the canal in water on the right. This is in the grounds of the Royal Horticultural Society's Rosemoor Gardens. If you walk a little further, the entrance is on the right. The restaurant/tea room is heartily recommended: Devon cream teas for a start.

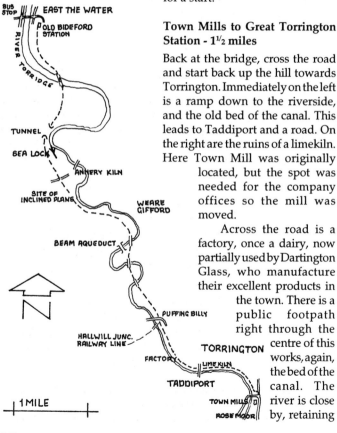

Town Mills to Great Torrington Station - 1¹/₂ miles

Back at the bridge, cross the road and start back up the hill towards Torrington. Immediately on the left is a ramp down to the riverside, and the old bed of the canal. This leads to Taddiport and a road. On the right are the ruins of a limekiln. Here Town Mill was originally located, but the spot was needed for the company offices so the mill was moved.

Across the road is a factory, once a dairy, now partially used by Dartington Glass, who manufacture their excellent products in the town. There is a public footpath right through the centre of this works, again, the bed of the canal. The river is close by, retaining the "water" aspect of this walk.

A railway bridge arrives from the left, and a flight of steps takes the walk up to this level. Note the road bridge ahead with two arches and the station buildings beyond. The railway was the Torrington to Hallwill Junction line of the Southern Railway. It lost its passenger service years ago, but was open until 1982 as far as Peters Marland, where a huge quarry produces ball clay for the pottery industry. Their original link with the national system was a privately owned narrow gauge line that met the standard gauge here: they used the right-hand arch.

Torrington Station to Annery Kilns - 3 miles

* After the railway finally closed, the local council turned the whole length into part of a long distance footpath, the Tarka Trail, which stretches for 180 miles around Devon. The old station is now a comfortable pub with huge log fires in winter. Following the railway north, it is only a few yards before the line of the canal is in use again. A boggy section on the right was the canal. As the river is crossed on a bridge, the canal curved off to the right, hugging the contour, only to come back across close to the next overbridge. It then crossed the river on a superb aqueduct which is in use today as part of a drive. An engraved stone on the north parapet tells of its construction. Now very overgrown, it appears to be inscribed thus:

THE FIRST STONE OF THIS AQUEDUCT WAS LAID BY THE RIGHT HONOURABLE JOHN LORD ROLLE BARON ROLLE OF STEVANSTONE IN THE COUNTY OF DEVON ON THE 11TH DAY OF AUGUST 1824 IN THE PRESENCE OF THE MAYOR CORPORATION AND ELECTORS OF GREAT TORRINGTON AND OF OTHER PERSONS ASSEMBLED TO WITNESS THE COMMENCEMENT OF THE CANAL UNDERTAKEN AT THE SOLE EXPENSE OF HIS LORDSHIP

JAMES GREEN ENGINEER.

This structure also achieved fame in a work of fiction. *Tarka the Otter* by Henry Williamson is a delightful wildlife tale. Early in the book, Tarka's mother is portrayed as living close to "the canal bridge", and around it, the young otter plays. This is it. On crossing the river again, a view of this structure can be obtained. It is also easily seen from the main road.

At grid reference SS 463225 was the site of the inclined plane at Ridds Cottage, but virtually all traces are now under the railway bed. The slope is still there, however. There is no documented evidence of how this incline was worked, but learned locals believe that a waterwheel was the power source. The fact that James Green used this idea on his Bude Canal would seem to increase that probability. The 40ft rise was achieved in just under 240ft, an incline of roughly 1 in 6.

Shortly beyond, the rail bed crosses a road. The housing a little to the right is Annery, and the large square building was a limekiln.

Annery to Bideford - 3 miles

The line of the canal - in water - can now be seen on the right. In a clump of trees, it joins the river at Sea Lock, map reference SS 458234, and the railway overlooks the site, albeit at some distance. Much of the masonry remains intact, although the original mouth is very silted.

Salmon are fished for in the river, and trespassers made very unwelcome. Here the company operated a boatyard where repairs to the canal's boats, barges and tubs were carried out. With laden barges arriving and unloading into trains of tub boats as well, this must once have been a very busy location. Sadly, all this aspect of the canal is no more.

As the river disappears to the right, the walk enters a short tunnel before returning waterside - more or less - for the rest of this walk. It is most unusual to be looking for cormorant and egret along this section rather than the more usual inland water birds. Approaching Bideford station, a local group have restored the station, its signal box and a little track. There is a carriage used as a tea room, and the whole ambience is excellent.

WALK 30 - EXETER TO TURF LOCK/ STARCROSS - EXETER CANAL

Down in deepest Devon, the Exeter Canal is alive. Although cut off from the main network, it still retains a modicum of trade, and provides a safe haven for seagoing boats. Perhaps not the most scenically attractive canal in the country, there is much of interest to compensate.

There are several conflicting claims to be the first canal in England. What is generally accepted is that the Exeter Canal was the first wholly artificial waterway to use pound locks. Navigation from Exeter to the English Channel appears to have gone on for as long as people had boats. But there have been turbulent times hereabouts. Back in 1282 Isabel, Countess of Devon, ordered a weir to be built across the River Exe at Topsham, below the city.

Topsham then became the port for Exeter until, after much legal wrangling, the weir was removed nearly 300 years later. By then the river had silted rather badly, and a canal was considered the easiest option. John Trew of Glamorgan cut a channel nearly 2 miles long to by-pass weirs. Sixteen feet wide and 3ft deep, it passed boats of up to 16 tons, but also provided "vertically rising sluices arranged in pairs".

Further improvements and lengthening took place under Richard Hurd between 1675, and 1698, when the whole canal was enlarged and a new lock built. James Green, this time with no need to build inclined planes, was in charge in 1821, and by 1830 the line was as it is today.

Exeter itself is a fine old city, deserving major exploration. The cathedral is magnificent, there are Roman remains, and a completely rebuilt town centre following Luftwaffe bombing on 4 May 1942. Much of the centre was razed, and over 400 shops and 36 pubs and clubs destroyed. The walk to the canal takes a slightly circuitous route to pass some of the more interesting bits.

BEFORE YOU START

WALK DISTANCE: 6 or 9 miles

MAP: OS Landranger Sheet 192

START: Swans Nest roundabout, Exminster, close to

Stepcote Hill in Exeter

	the end of the M5 on the A379 Exeter to Dawlish road
PUBLIC TRANSPORT:	Exeter is well served by coach and train
STARTING GRID REF:	SX 951872
CAR PARKING:	Lane to the east of the island near the Swan Inn
TRANSPORT:	Devon General services 85, 85A and 85B. Enquiries on 01392 56231
REFRESHMENT:	Everything in Exeter, two pubs en route
NEAREST TIC:	Civic Centre, Paris Street, Exeter, Devon EX1 1JJ - 01392 265700

THE WALK

There is a choice to be made right at the start. For the shorter walk, return to the main road and turn left. Across, a few yards along, is the bus stop. Catch the service to Exeter bus station.

Walk along the station concourse, turn left down a flight of steps into Paris Street and right up the hill. At the top, with Debenhams and Dillons opposite, turn left into High Street. Continue along here and pick up the narrative at *

For the longer walk:

Exminster to Topsham - 4 miles

Walk down the lane past the Swan Inn until it reaches the canal. Turn right. Open flood plains predominate as the walk heads south. After a mile moored boats will be found above the sea lock, and an inn, the Turf, hard by. Whether this is a lonely abandoned outpost or vibrant centre of interest depends on whether you visit in summer or winter. In recent years it has closed out of season. The sea lock and landing stage below are all in full working order.

The path continues alongside the estuary for just over a mile. Here, a level crossing takes the walk to the other side of the railway. Be careful: this is a high speed railway.

Continue along the estuary - albeit with the railway between - to Starcross station. On the right is Powderham Castle, still privately owned but open to visitors. The parklands hold over 700 fallow deer, and they are usually visible.

On reaching the station there is a choice of routes back to Exeter.

The fun way - in summer only - is to take the ferry across the water to Exmouth and catch a train from there to Exeter Central. There is also a service from Starcross to Central, or the bus service mentioned earlier runs along this road.

By Train:
Leave Exeter Central and turn left. At the first major crossroads, turn right.

By Bus:
Follow directions for the "shorter" walk given in the "START" section.

All Together Now:

* The Guildhall is on the right. This is the oldest functioning municipal building in the country. Built in 1330, it was improved in 1468, whilst the portico was added during the reign of Elizabeth I in about 1594. The Turks Head pub, next-door, is a delightfully quaint and tiny building.

High Street becomes Fore Street. Note the interesting old building on the right, Tuckers Hall. Built in 1490 for the Guild of Weavers, Fullers and Shearmen, this ancient guild still functions today, one of

"The House that Moved" is just that. Originally sited 400 yards away, a new road went through its original site. Not wanting to lose such a wonderful building, it was carefully transported to this site

the few left outside the city of London. A "tucker", incidentally, was another name for a fuller.

Turn around and walk back up Fore Street for a few yards until reaching King Street on the right. Take that turn and the first right again. This is Stepcote Hill, a delightful cobbled street of medieval appearance, with stepped walkway and central run-off for rain water - and whatever else was tipped into the streets in previous centuries! At the bottom is the House that Moved. Originally located in Edmund Street, close by, it was in the way of a new road scheme in 1961. Rather than demolish such a treasure, the whole structure was moved on rollers to its present site, close to West Gate. This corner is a delight, with a couple of very old shops, and St. Mary's Church adding a little dignity to an otherwise

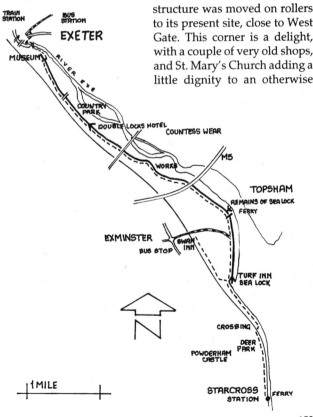

frivolous scene.

Walk towards the new road and cross the first carriageway before turning right. This leads over what was once the Exe bridge with gatehouse. Turn left and at the end go under the subway and turn right up the slope. This brings the walk to the current course of the River Exe.

Turn left along the bank. After 150 yards cross the metal Cricklepit Bridge to the right bank and turn left. The new town houses here are stark contrast to the dereliction that reigned here for so many years, and is only now being tackled.

As the river turns to the right, the Exeter Maritime Museum comes into view. Directly ahead in the ground is some railway track and an old wagon turntable. This was part of a short goods railway to City Basin built by the South Devon Railway in 1867. Originally it used Brunel's broad (7ft) gauge, but in 1871 a third rail was added to allow standard gauge London and South West Railway traffic to use it.

The buildings here and across the river are some of the best preserved in the country. A television series *The Onedin Line* was shot here because if offered the most authentic settings. The first brick house in Exeter was built here in 1681 as Customs House, now an Ancient Monument, and still used by Customs and Excise.

Maritime Museum to Countess Wear Bridge - 2 miles

Walk to the right of the basin, keeping to the water's edge. The now derelict buildings were once the home of Exeter Maritime Museum. Sadly, the place closed in 1996 after 27 years on the site.

The path leads away from the water, past modern boats on hard standing and the River and Canal Office. Here swing bridges cross the head of the basin and Kings Arm Sluice. This gate prevents flood water from the Exe entering the canal. The gas offices on the left are where the old gasworks once stood. This was the last works in the south west to make gas from coal before the arrival of the natural variety. The original plant was sited here in 1836, and the last edifice demolished in 1973.

An excellent towpath here makes walking easy at first. It is paved, and stays that way for quite a way. On the water there is usually a good selection of seabirds, certainly not the type usually associated with canals. The view to the right is of the eastern edge of Dartmoor.

Double Locks Hotel comes into view before too long, but first the canal passes the most enormous lock chamber. Almost like a pound between the gates, it measures some 300ft long and about 100ft across at its widest point. The balance beams are enormous tubular steel pipes. The hotel itself offers a break, and has lots of trees in its garden, with children's playground and a barbecue.

Beyond, Countess Wear Bascule Bridge crosses the canal carrying a fiendishly busy road. This has to be crossed, but fortunately there is a central reservation to help.

Countess Wear Bridge to Topsham Ferry - 2 miles

The towpath now turns to what one considers normal: muddy but walkable. The river closes in tight to the left-hand bank after a further ¹/₄ mile. The causeway between gives car access to South West Water's Water Treatment Plant; a modern euphemism for sewage works. Hereabouts was the original southern terminus of the canal, but there is no evidence left today of where it joined the river.

The works across extends quite a long way, and the canal widens considerably. Round the corner is the sole remnant of trade. A ship, the *Countess Wear* moors here, loads treated sludge from the works and takes it out to sea for dumping. How long it will be before this last commercial traffic is floored remains to be seen.

The noisy M5 passes overhead on a long viaduct as the walk approaches Topsham Ferry. Just above, on the far side of the canal, can be seen the remains of a sea lock that was the entrance to the canal for many years before the southern extension was built in 1832. On completion, it enabled craft to reach the canal at all stages of the tide. The chamber is still more or less intact, and the paddle gear in place. Another restoration project?

Topsham Ferry to Turf lock - 1¹/₂ miles

After ¹/₂ mile the Starcross walkers will recognise the point where they joined the towpath. Turn right here to return to the Swan Inn. The shorter walk continues along the towpath to the Turf Inn, where the canal joins the sea. Cross the stile to the west of the chamber, and head towards the railway before bearing right. This footpath will take you back to a bridge. Cross it, and the Swan Inn is just beyond.

* * *

CICERONE GUIDES
Cicerone publish a wide range of reliable guides to walking and climbing in Britain, and other general interest books.

LAKE DISTRICT - General Books
CONISTON COPPER A History
CHRONICLES OF MILNTHORPE
A DREAM OF EDEN -LAKELAND DALES
EDEN TAPESTRY
THE HIGH FELLS OF LAKELAND
KENDAL A SOCIAL HISTORY
LAKELAND - A taste to remember (Recipes)
LAKELAND VILLAGES
LAKELAND TOWNS
LAKELAND PANORAMAS
THE LAKERS
THE LOST RESORT? (Morecambe)
LOST LANCASHIRE (Furness area)
REFLECTIONS ON THE LAKES
AN ILLUSTRATED COMPANION INTO LAKELAND

LAKE DISTRICT - Guide Books
THE BORDERS OF LAKELAND
BIRDS OF MORECAMBE BAY
CASTLES IN CUMBRIA
CONISTON COPPER MINES Field Guide
THE CUMBRIA CYCLE WAY
THE CUMBRIA WAY & ALLERDALE RAMBLE
THE EDEN WAY
IN SEARCH OF WESTMORLAND
SHORT WALKS IN LAKELAND-1: SOUTH LAKELAND
SHORT WALKS IN LAKELAND- 2:NORTH LAKELAND
SCRAMBLES IN THE LAKE DISTRICT
MORE SCRAMBLES IN THE LAKE DISTRICT
THE TARNS OF LAKELAND VOL 1 - WEST
THE TARNS OF LAKELAND VOL 2 - EAST
WALKING ROUND THE LAKES
WALKS IN SILVERDALE/ARNSIDE
WESTMORLAND HERITAGE WALK
WINTER CLIMBS IN THE LAKE DISTRICT

NORTHERN ENGLAND (outside the Lakes
BIRDWATCHING ON MERSEYSIDE
CANAL WALKS Vol 1 North
CANOEISTS GUIDE TO THE NORTH EAST
THE CLEVELAND WAY & MISSING LINK
THE DALES WAY

DOUGLAS VALLEY WAY
FAMILY WALKS IN BOWLAND
WALKING IN THE FOREST OF BOWLAND
HADRIANS WALL Vol 1 The Wall Walk
HADRIANS WALL VOL 2 Walks around the Wall
HERITAGE TRAILS IN NW ENGLAND
THE ISLE OF MAN COASTAL PATH
IVORY TOWERS & DRESSED STONES (Follies)
THE LANCASTER CANAL
LANCASTER CANAL WALKS
A WALKERS GUIDE TO THE LANCASTER CANAL
WALKS FROM THE LEEDS-LIVERPOOL CANAL
LAUGHS ALONG THE PENNINE WAY
A NORTHERN COAST-TO-COAST
NORTH YORK MOORS Walks
ON THE RUFFSTUFF 84 Bike rides in Northern England
THE REIVERS WAY (Northumberland)
THE RIBBLE WAY
THE TEESDALE WAY
WALKING IN COUNTY DURHAM
WALKING IN LANCASHIRE
WALKING DOWN THE LUNE
WALKING IN THE SOUTH PENNINES
WALKING IN THE NORTH PENNINES
WALKING IN THE WOLDS
WALKS IN THE YORKSHIRE DALES (3 VOL)
WALKS IN LANCASHIRE WITCH COUNTRY
WALKS IN THE NORTH YORK MOORS (2 VOL)
WALKS TO YORKSHIRE WATERFALLS (2 vol)
WATERFALL WALKS -TEESDALE & THE HIGH PENNINES
WALKS ON THE WEST PENNINE MOORS
WALKING NORTHERN RAILWAYS (2 vol)
THE YORKSHIRE DALES A walker's guide

DERBYSHIRE PEAK DISTRICT & EAST MIDLANDS
KINDER LOG
HIGH PEAK WALKS
WHITE PEAK WAY
WHITE PEAK WALKS - 2 Vols
WEEKEND WALKS IN THE PEAK DISTRICT
THE VIKING WAY
THE DEVIL'S MILL / WHISTLING CLOUGH (Novels)

Other guides are constantly being added to the Cicerone List.
Available from bookshops, outdoor equipment shops or direct (send s.a.e. for price list) from
CICERONE, 2 POLICE SQUARE, MILNTHORPE, CUMBRIA, LA7 7PY

CICERONE GUIDES
Cicerone publish a wide range of reliable guides to walking and climbing in Britain, and other general interest books.

WALES, WELSH BORDER & WEST MIDLANDS
ASCENT OF SNOWDON
THE BRECON BEACONS
WALKING IN CHESHIRE
THE CHESHIRE CYCLE WAY
CLWYD ROCK
HEREFORD & THE WYE VALLEY A Walker's Guide
HILLWALKING IN SNOWDONIA
HILL WALKING IN WALES (2 Vols)
THE LLEYN PENINSULA COASTAL PATH
THE MOUNTAINS OF ENGLAND & WALES Vol 1
WALES
WALKING OFFA'S DYKE PATH
THE RIDGES OF SNOWDONIA
ROCK CLIMBS IN WEST MIDLANDS
SARN HELEN Walking Roman Road
SCRAMBLES IN SNOWDONIA
SEVERN WALKS
THE SHROPSHIRE HILLS A Walker's Guide
SNOWDONIA WHITE WATER SEA & SURF
WALKING DOWN THE WYE
A WELSH COAST TO COAST WALK
WELSH WINTER CLIMBS

SOUTH & SOUTH WEST ENGLAND
WALKING IN CORNWALL
WALKING IN THE CHILTERNS
COTSWOLD WAY
COTSWOLD WALKS (3 VOLS)
WALKING ON DARTMOOR
WALKERS GUIDE TO DARTMOOR PUBS
WALKING IN DEVON
WALKING IN DORSET
EXMOOR & THE QUANTOCKS
THE GRAND UNION CANAL WALK
THE KENNET & AVON WALK
LONDON THEME WALKS
WALKING IN OXFORDSHIRE
AN OXBRIDGE WALK
A SOUTHERN COUNTIES BIKE GUIDE
THE SOUTHERN-COAST-TO-COAST

SOUTH DOWNS WAY & DOWNS LINK
SOUTH WEST WAY - 2 Vol
THE TWO MOORS WAY Dartmoor-Exmoor
WALKS IN KENT Bk 2
THE WEALDWAY & VANGUARD WAY

SCOTLAND
THE BORDER COUNTRY - WALKERS GUIDE
BORDER PUBS & INNS A Walker's Guide
CAIRNGORMS WINTER CLIMBS
WALKING THE GALLOWAY HILLS
THE ISLAND OF RHUM
THE ISLE OF SKYE - A Walker's Guide
THE SCOTTISH GLENS (Mountainbike Guide)
   Book 1:THE CAIRNGORM GLENS
   Book 2 THE ATHOLL GLENS
   Book 3 THE GLENS OF RANNOCH
   Book 4 THE GLENS OF TROSSACH
   Book 5 THE GLENS OF ARGYLL
   Book 6 THE GREAT GLEN
SCOTTISH RAILWAY WALKS
SCRAMBLES IN LOCHABER
SCRAMBLES IN SKYE
SKI TOURING IN SCOTLAND
TORRIDON A Walker's Guide
WALKS from the WEST HIGHLAND RAILWAY
WINTER CLIMBS BEN NEVIS & GLENCOE

REGIONAL BOOKS UK & IRELAND
THE ALTERNATIVE PENNINE WAY
THE ALTERNATIVE COAST TO COAST
LANDS END TO JOHN O'GROATS CYCLE GUIDE
CANAL WALKS Vol.1: North
CANAL WALKS Vol.2: Midlands
CANAL WALKS Vol.3: South
LIMESTONE - 100 BEST CLIMBS
THE PACKHORSE BRIDGES OF ENGLAND
THE RELATIVE HILLS OF BRITAIN
THE MOUNTAINS OF ENGLAND & WALES
   VOL 1 WALES, VOL 2 ENGLAND
THE MOUNTAINS OF IRELAND
THE IRISH COAST TO COAST WALK

Also a full range of EUROPEAN and OVERSEAS guidebooks - walking, long distance trails,
scrambling, ice-climbing, rock climbing.

Other guides are constantly being added to the Cicerone List.
Available from bookshops, outdoor equipment shops or direct (send s.a.e. for price list) from
CICERONE, 2 POLICE SQUARE, MILNTHORPE, CUMBRIA, LA7 7PY

PRINTED BY CARNMOR PRINT & DESIGN
LONDON ROAD, PRESTON, PR1 4BA, UK